Totally amazing. This book p̲   ̲it
missionaries might encounter ar̲   ̲t
you follow in the Lord's leading   s
life interesting and rewarding.

You will want to get to the e̲n̲d̲ ̲o̲f̲ ̲t̲h̲e̲ ̲b̲o̲o̲k̲,̲ ̲b̲u̲t̲ ̲y̲o̲u̲
don't really want it to end. It's music for the soul that we can trust God even against the intentions of the devil and our own doubts.

This book has given such insight of God's loving care and his answering of prayer, and a greater appreciation of the life of missionary "Hermano Dónal" in his desire to humbly follow in the will of God.

—Roy and Leona Nielsen

What an encouragement this memoir has been to read! It is beautifully written and the suspense of what is to come is exciting.

—Erika Stewart

I really like all the details… One can feel the heat and the itches, imagine the tin can "cup," etc. I just love hearing all of these stories.

—Michelle Strutzenberger

Thank you, Don. I can surely see the Lord's leading and power in the ministry He called you to. Bless you for your faithful obedience… you're a real encouragement to me!

—Pastor Morris Mills

It is wonderful to see the way the Lord works out his plans step by step. This book leaves a good testimony of the Lord.

—Jim Stanley

I was going to read the pages slowly, but they are so interesting and written so well. I read it all and wished for more. Absolutely terrific!

—Carolyn Reimer

Thank you so very much for allowing me to read your memoirs of Costa Rica. It is most exciting and uplifting to read just how our wonderful God works in every situation when we allow Him to answer our prayers.

—Pat Moore

An Autobiography by
Don Dodsworth

FOLLOWING GOD'S LEAD IN THE WILDERNESS
Copyright © 2023 by Donald Dodsworth

All rights reserved. Neither this publication nor any part of this publication may be reproduced or transmitted in any form or by any means, electronic or mechanical, including photocopying, recording or any information storage and retrieval system, without permission in writing from the author.

Unless otherwise indicated, all scripture quotations taken from the Holy Bible, King James Version, which is in the public domain. Scripture quotations marked "NKJV" taken from the New King James Version®. Copyright © 1982 by Thomas Nelson. Used by permission. All rights reserved. Scripture quotations marked "RSV" taken from the Revised Standard Version of the Bible, copyright © 1946, 1952, and 1971 the Division of Christian Education of the National Council of the Churches of Christ in the United States of America. Used by permission. All rights reserved. Scripture quotations marked "ESV" are from The ESV® Bible (The Holy Bible, English Standard Version®), copyright © 2001 by Crossway, a publishing ministry of Good News Publishers. Used by permission. All rights reserved.

ISBN: 978-1-4866-2383-9
eBook ISBN: 978-1-4866-2384-6

Word Alive Press
119 De Baets Street Winnipeg, MB R2J 3R9
www.wordalivepress.ca

Cataloguing in Publication information can be obtained from Library and Archives Canada.

ACKNOWLEDGEMENTS

I certainly owe a lot of gratitude to my wife Grace who, while she could, worked on editing the first chapters of this memoir.

I must also thank Leona Nielsen, who worked hard to help with editing of the manuscript.

I also make special mention of Michelle Strutzenberger, who has done the most of anyone to encourage me to publish these memoirs into a book. She continued to encourage me as I completed more chapters.

Jim Stanley, a full-time missionary to Senegal and Guinea in West Africa, also made a strong plea for me to have this book printed.

Many others, including my sister-in-law Mary Edwards, encouraged me as well. A number of people made very encouraging remarks about different parts of the manuscript and I thank them.

I would also like to thank Word Alive Press for their tremendous help in the process of making this book a reality. Thank you Evan Braun for your patience with me and your expertise in the editing of this manuscript. Also thank you Crystal Hildebrand, as the project manager, for such a gentle and loving spirit to see me through this.

CONTENTS

ACKNOWLEDGEMENTS	V
One: DON'S GOING TO COSTA RICA	1
Two: A CHANCE ACQUAINTANCE	5
Three: A TRIP TO COSTA RICA	9
Four: FIRST VISIT TO THE MALEKU	15
Five: PREPARING TO RETURN TO COSTA RICA	21
Six: COSTA RICA, HERE WE COME	25
Seven: GOD'S LEADING TO THE MALEKU	31
Eight: EARLY DAYS IN COSTA RICA	35
Nine: BAPTISM	43
Ten: THE MALEKU MINISTRY	47
Eleven: RETURNING HOME	55
Twelve: PLANE CRASH	61
Thirteen: CHAINSAW WORK AND HORSE TRAVEL	65
Fourteen: GAINING TRUST AND EVEN DEPENDENCE	71

Fifteen: FRUSTRATION, DISCOURAGEMENT, ILLNESS, AND QUESTIONS	79
Sixteen: A SKEPTICAL FARMER	83
Seventeen: EARTHQUAKE	89
Eighteen: AMOEBAS AND BUENAVISTA	95
Nineteen: STRETCHING OUR FAITH	99
Twenty: A BULL ON THE LOOSE	105
Twenty-One: OFF TO NICARAGUA	107
Twenty-Two: CAYUCO GOES MISSING	115
Twenty-Three: MAKING A DUGOUT CANOE	119
Twenty-Four: A DIFFERENT WAY TO GUATUSO	127
Twenty-Five: MY FOURTH TRIP SOUTH	131
Twenty-Six: BACK FOR THE BUS	141
Twenty-Seven: WHAT DO I DO NOW LORD?	147
Twenty-Eight: THE OLD COLONY MENNONITES OF BLUE CREEK	151
Twenty-Nine: UNA COMPAÑERA	155
Thirty: IS THAT MAN GOING TO SHOW UP OR NOT?	161
CONCLUSION	171
ABOUT THE AUTHOR	173

DON'S GOING TO COSTA RICA
Summer 1968

But seek ye first the kingdom of God, and his righteousness; and all these things shall be added unto you. (Matthew 6:33)

"Don's going to Costa Rica."

The sound of these words shook me to my boots. I had been thinking out loud when I'd mentioned to my older brother that I believed God was calling me to join some missionaries and accompany them in their mission field in Costa Rica. I had taken a two-week trip to Costa Rica, but now I was thinking of going back to stay for a much longer time.

The reality of the idea hit me when I heard the plan spoken back to me, and I wondered at this point if I should have ever mentioned it. I hadn't even told my parents yet. What if they found out from someone else first?

Was I sure about going? Did I really sense God's leading or was it just me thinking that God wanted me to do this?

I had been praying about God's plan for my life ever since I had come back from Costa Rica. That trip had left a lasting impression, as well as a concern as to what it meant for my future. At that point, I'd had no thoughts of ever being a missionary, but what was the significance of the precise way in which God had worked out the details of the trip in such surprising ways? Henry Teigrob and myself had experienced numerous delays in the preparations for our trip, first during our travel to Montreal by car and then on the flight to Costa Rica. Yet, as precise as clockwork, every detail had worked out in the nick of time.

In Costa Rica, my eyes were opened to an opportunity to share the gospel, but I had thought that opportunity must surely be meant for someone else. It definitely wasn't for me. I was a trained electronic technician and that's what I had expected to be doing for the rest of my life.

Maybe God wanted me to encourage others to go and be missionaries? Although I realized I had never been a very persuasive person in getting others to do things.

I prayed for more knowledge of the Bible and to discover where to get help in learning God's word.

While listening to a message on leadership, something really clicked. That trip to Costa Rica came to mind. By watching how Henry had committed every matter to prayer then, as cool as a cucumber trusting God to answer, I had learned something about trusting God in a practical way. This confidence in God amazed me.

If I studied the Bible by myself, without help, I might learn slowly. But with help I could learn so much faster. I knew I needed leadership in trusting God at his word. Who could recommend where I should go to learn more from the Bible? I didn't just want a head knowledge of the Bible; I wanted to be instructed by someone who fully believed God is able to be present where the rubber grips the road.

As I pondered how God was trying to lead me, a question came to mind. *Is God trying to tell me that Brother Henry could be my instructor if I joined him on the mission field?* I had only gone to Costa Rica for a vacation, but there had been too much direct intervention on the trip for it to be *just* a vacation. Had all those obstacles along the way, marvellously rectified in such precise timing, occurred for no reason?

The more I thought about this, the more it seemed to ring true.

A few months after returning to Canada, I had visited the Teigrob family and told them what I was thinking.

"Let's pray about it," Henry had said, although he didn't talk any more about it at the time.

Now I was shaken because I had told my oldest brother and he was telling others. Was I really able to follow through with this plan? Was I convinced that God was leading me in it? Such a decision would mean giving up my career as an electronic technician, after just finishing my training.

What about my family and friends? What would they think of this? And since I wasn't being sent out by a mission, would they worry about my well-being?

Two

A CHANCE ACQUAINTANCE
1963–Summer 1967

In the small Nova Scotian village of Fort Lawrence, my folks raised a few cattle on a farm. The village got its name from a fort the English had used many years ago, when the English and French had fought for what was the "new land." About all that's left of the fort today is the name.

I lived in Fort Lawrence while in high school and picked up a number of practical skills while working on our farm and on some of the neighbours' farms. At seventeen, I had been more than anxious to get my driver's licence. However, dad seldom found time for me to practice driving and a "learner" was only allowed to drive when no one else was in the vehicle except the one responsible.

One day, my brother Bill asked if I wanted to go Moncton, New Brunswick to hear a Presbyterian minister named Leighton Ford speak at a crusade. I didn't want to go, but I realized that if I agreed he might let me drive partway.

"Sure," I replied.

And I wasn't disappointed.

However, Ford's message, to my surprise, hit me in a way that the Scriptures hadn't. He emphasized that one can't be a private Christian. I knew, in reality, that this is what I really was—a private Christian—and that I needed to stand up for Jesus. If I couldn't take a stand for Him amongst all these strangers, where could I ever stand for Him?

I went forward at the invitation and soon learned of a number of scriptures that supported Ford's message but which until now had not registered in my understanding. For example, Matthew 10:33: *"but whoever denies me before men, I also will deny before my Father who is in heaven"* (RSV).

God became real to me after that. My faith increased as I studied His Word and continued to take steps of faith as I felt nudged to do so.

After graduating from high school, I moved to Halifax to train as an electronic technician at HMS Dockyard. I travelled home once every two or three weeks to spend the weekend with Mom and Dad.

My paternal grandparents lived about halfway between Fort Lawrence and Halifax, and since their place was only a short distance off the main highway I occasionally took the time to stop in and visit. I did this for their sake, since they seemed to appreciate my visits even more than I did.

One of my visits happened to be close to church time. A missionary named Henry Teigrob was helping out at their church and my grandparents wanted me to hear him speak. I wasn't interested in hearing any missionary, but I wanted to make them happy by going to church with them. The speaker really impressed me and he spoke as though God was real to him.

Afterward my grandparents asked what I thought of the message. I told them I wanted to hear Henry speak again, although I didn't think that would be a possibility.

"Why don't you come back next week?" my grandmother asked.

The thought of me driving more than an hour each way just to hear a message seemed outrageous.

Nevertheless, I was there the next Sunday. Also, my grandparents had something up their sleeve that I didn't know about. They had invited Henry and his wife Anne to come to their house for supper after the service. I think they wanted me to have some time to talk with the Teigrobs, which surely I did.

That afternoon, Henry made the suggestion that since I visited my grandparents at times I might stop in and see them as well. They, too, only lived a short distance off the main highway. What could I say?

The day soon came when I decided to stop by and pay them a visit. They just happened to be showing slides of Costa Rica with another family who was visiting at the time.

I found the pictures to be extraordinarily beautiful.

"What a beautiful place to visit!" I remarked. "I could go there on my next vacation."

Since I had already been all across Canada, this place looked very enticing. But then reality set in. I didn't know why I had blurted out such a stupid idea. How would I ever manage to get by in a Spanish-speaking country? I quickly dropped the idea.

Two weeks later, I heard a knock on my apartment door in Halifax. It was Henry!

Not only was I surprised to see him, but I was even more surprised about what he had to say. He was going down to Costa Rica, where he and Anne had worked as missionaries, for a two-week visit. Then, in a year, he would be returning with the whole family.

"Would you like to go with me?" he asked.

Wow! I didn't have to think twice about it. I don't think I even prayed about it. What an opportunity it would be to travel with someone who could translate for me…

Yes, sure, I would go! The trip was to be the experience of a lifetime.

Three

A TRIP TO COSTA RICA

How soon would this trip be? What did I need to do to get ready? Henry was leaving in four weeks and I needed a passport, which sometimes could take six weeks to process, plus various vaccinations and booster shots. We prayed about these things.

I was quite sure the Dockyard would give me the two-week vacation time on short notice, which they did. That meant I could proceed with the rest of my plans. I processed the passport application in two days and sent it off. The required vaccination shots could be scheduled in the four weeks, but it would be close.

As a real answer to prayer, I received my passport in ten days. Our passports also required visas for Costa Rica. Henry gave our passports to the travel agent to send to the consulate in Montreal.

Regarding our travel route, Henry suggested that it would be cheapest to drive to Montreal, then fly to Costa Rica via Miami. However, he encountered some difficulties trying to reserve the flights through a travel agent. I offered to try my hand at it, booking directly through Air Canada's office in Halifax. Not only did this work, but they offered cheaper flights than the ones Henry had obtained.

Later there was a mix-up in the process of booking the cheaper tickets, and that mix-up didn't get resolved until the very day we were to leave for Montreal.

My car was almost new, so I offered to use it to get to Montreal. Henry had an old VW van he had just purchased, and he had no idea what bugs it might have. The other big difference between the two vehicles—one was entirely paid for and the other, well, the bank had a share in it.

"We'll take the one that is paid for," Henry said as a matter of principle.

On Friday morning, the day we wanted to leave for Montreal, I proceeded to Henry's place only to discover from him that the passports still hadn't arrived.

"Let's go into town to check with the travel agent," he suggested.

Sure enough, they were there, praise the Lord. We had an early supper and got ready to head out for Montreal.

After praying together with the family, Henry and I headed out on the highway. We hadn't gone far before Henry began to notice a shimmy on the steering wheel. We stopped at a garage on the Tantamar Marsh just past Amherst. The mechanic informed us that the suspension badly needed grease, but also that a few parts might need replacing as well. He advised us to have an alignment mechanic look at it.

After a mechanic in Amherst inspected the vehicle, he told us that the van needed quite a major amount of work. It was now 5:00 p.m. on a Friday, though, and the mechanic was finished work for the week. He told us that he would get to it on Monday morning.

Wow!

Everything stops here, I thought. *The trip is over.*

What Henry said next blew me away. "You know that the front tire is low on air. What if we go back to the first mechanic to get him to grease up the front suspension? Then we can pump up that tire and see if it runs any better."

THREE: A TRIP TO COSTA RICA

"We could try it," I said, trying not to be a doubter. But I hardly had an ounce of faith.

Nevertheless, the shimmy totally disappeared as we got going again. Thankfully, we were back on our way.

That was only the beginning of our troubles.

As night drew on, the air in the van got colder. Henry knew that the gasoline heater required a piece of tubing to connect the gas line to the heater. We stopped at a number of garages along the way until we finally found one that could supply us with the needed piece of hose. Heat at last! Or perhaps I should say it was slightly warmed air; it didn't even warm the car enough for us to remove the blankets we had wrapped ourselves in.

Then a headlight went out. We fixed it and carried on. Then the other one went out. We fixed that one and continued. Then, can you believe it, both headlights went out?

After travelling a little in the dark, Henry spotted yet another garage. He got the headlights fixed and we went on our way again.

Through the night, we shivered in the cold—and finally, at six o'clock in the morning, we stopped for coffee.

I took over the driving with the sun rising over my left shoulder. The sun's rays permeated my shoulder and slowly warmed the rest of my upper body.

Later, as Henry was driving, smoke started billowing up from under the dash and all went dead. We coasted at highway speed while I desperately tried to find the source of the smoke.

Suddenly, Henry saw another garage and we coasted the vehicle off the highway and up to the garage doors. The mechanic figured that the problem had to do with the gas heater's wiring.

With the sun up, we could now manage without the heater. So the mechanic disconnected the heater, replaced some fuses, and sent us on our way.

I must say that Henry remained calm throughout this saga and never appeared to worry about whether we would get to Montreal on time. Indeed, we rolled into the airport an hour and a half before our plane was due to leave.

11

Next thing we knew, we were flying south for Miami.

After disembarking at Miami, our next step was to retrieve our luggage. Miami's international airport was very large, however, and we went off in the wrong direction looking for Air Canada's luggage pickup. By the time we found it, all the other passengers had retrieved their luggage and only two pieces of luggage remained. They looked like ours…

"That's not my luggage," Henry remarked as we approached.

To me, it looked identical to the bag Henry had checked back in Montreal. But Henry had immediately noticed an odd nameplate.

We turned the luggage in to Lost and Found, where we discovered that they would only be open for two more hours. After that, they'd be closed until 8:00 a.m.

However, our flight for Costa Rica was departing at 5:30 a.m.

Henry had a connection with some people who ran a seniors citizens home and nursing facility not too far from the airport, and they offered us the privilege to stay overnight. At the cottage where we were given lodging, we prayed for wisdom in what to do. We were almost too exhausted from the heat to think clearly.

We asked the Lord to guide us. Should we fly the next day without luggage or postpone our flight by one day in the hopes that our luggage could be found? Before the Lord, we decided that if the people who had taken the wrong luggage managed to return it within the next two hours, we would continue to Costa Rica as scheduled.

Guess what? The luggage was returned on time and sent to us by taxi.

We had only slept a couple of hours and I desperately wanted to catch up on some sleep. Henry, however, wanted me to go with him and talk to the staff at the adjacent nursing home. He wanted to track down some acquaintances of his.

We found his friends and talked with them until midnight.

"You probably haven't had any supper," one of the nurses exclaimed. We looked at each other, laughed, and said nothing. "Just sit still. We have lots of leftovers."

THREE: A TRIP TO COSTA RICA

She proceeded to lay out a meal before us. It was 1:00 a.m. before we went to bed and we got up again at 3:00 to catch a taxi to the airport. Despite the short sleep, we were surprisingly refreshed.

The central plain in Costa Rica, where the majority of the country's people live, sits four thousand feet above sea level and the weather is, more or less, like a Canadian summer all year around.

From the airport, we took a bus to the capital city of San José and looked up the Mennonite centre. Henry was a member of a Mennonite Brethren church, so he always had connections with evangelical Mennonite groups.

We spent the night at the centre and then boarded a bus for San Carlos the following day. Halfway along the five-hour trip north, the bus stopped for a short break. We didn't get off, but a young boy came on board to sell his wares.

"Buy some of these," Henry said of a type of palm fruit the boy was selling. "They're good."

I bought a half-dozen for both of us and asked what they were called.

"Pejibayes," he replied.

However, after having travelled quite a while already over a rough and mountainous highway, my stomach was feeling queasy. These pejibayes smelt like cooked squash and I had to get away from them. I gave mine to Henry and moved to the other side of the bus.

Our travel had started at four thousand feet of altitude, but we climbed above six thousand feet before winding back down a twisty road to arrive at Ciudad Quesada. We found the hotel we had booked, although it didn't quite fit the description we had read about in Canada. It looked more like someone's beach cabin than a hotel! I made a comment about it and Henry replied, "Cheer up. Worse is yet to come."

I noticed later on that this was a phrase he often used.

The next day we visited with a number of Henry's acquaintances. They conversed in a language I didn't know. I realized I would have to get used to listening for long hours to conversations that didn't make a bit of sense to me. This would be my lot for most of the next ten days. After all, with so many people for Henry to talk to, there wasn't much time left for Henry and I to converse.

Pejibaye trees resemble a palm tree but have long thorns on the trunks from top to bottom. They need a long pole with a 'y' stick on the end to bring the fruit down

Four

FIRST VISIT TO THE MALEKU

Early in the morning, we made our way to the Ciudad Quesada airstrip. We booked a flight to Guatuso, which was one hour's walk from the nearest palenque.[1] However, it could take much longer if it was the wet season or you weren't acclimatized to the high temperature and humidity.

After a twenty-minute flight, we landed on a grass strip. As soon as the four-seater plane came to a halt and the door was opened, the air hit us like a wave of air from a hot oven. Wow! The altitude here was close to sea level.

Since we would need sombreros to keep our heads cool, we walked to the nearest general store. The lady there knew Henry and offered us a refreshing drink straight away. We purchased our sombreros along with some cookies and fruit drinks.

We then headed out on a jungle trail. It was the dry season but we weren't accustomed to this heat. A green snake slithered across the

---

1 The native villages were all called palenques and most Costa Ricans referred to these people as Guatusans.

pathway and up an embankment. It was thin but longer than any snake I'd ever seen, at least ten feet long.

We hadn't gone far, distance wise, when Henry suggested we stop for a break. I agreed. We then trudged on through the jungle and came to a river, where we took off our shoes and wadded across. After clambering up the bank on the other side, we came to the first palenque, called El Sol, meaning "the sun."

That first view of the villagers' homes left a lasting impression on me. They were all leaf-roofed and had neither floor nor even side walls. The cats, dogs, pigs, chickens, and whatever other animals they had roamed in and out of their dwellings at will. They had some poor hammocks and tree bark on the ground to sleep on at night.

As I stood on the sidelines just inside the hut, some black flying insects got entangled in my hair. When I was told that they were bees, I grew concerned. Henry translated to me that they wouldn't sting. Still, I moved to another spot, keeping an eye out for them.

After what seemed to me like a long time, the people offered us something to eat. A small table about three feet long, made from a slab of wood fastened to two posts planted in the ground, stood at the end of the hut. Its bench was built in a similar fashion. We were given black coffee and some toasted bread twists with some pejibayes on metallic plates coated with enamel.

Because of my earlier experience on the bus, I passed my pejibayes straight over to Henry. My coffee was served in a large aluminum mug, but Henry's was given to him in an old oil can. I hoped it didn't have sharp edges that might cut his lips.

As I ate the bread twists, I began to wonder how long it might be before I got something else to eat. Henry had stressed to me the importance of eating what grew in the area because God had put it there for some purpose.

"Can you give me a piece of pejibaye for me to try?" I said to Henry.

I ate a piece and found that it didn't taste too bad. I ate more, and from then on I had no problem eating them.

FOUR: FIRST VISIT TO THE MALEKU

We soon moved on to the next palenque, Margarita. At our arrival the whole village came out to greet us, shaking our hands from the oldest to the youngest. It was quite an exciting moment!

These people had a custom that made us chuckle, yet we understood what they meant by it. They began by asking when we were going to leave. Also, as a custom, when we were leaving they further asked when we were going to return.

This palenque was a little more advanced, with wooden huts and metallic roofs. The government had sent in a contractor to supervise the building of the houses. He'd come with a chainsaw and cut down trees which he then cut into boards. With the natives' help, they had built their houses with these boards, including floors. They also built lean-to sheds next to their homes to use as kitchens, which had palm-thatched roofs and mud floors. The leaf roofs were much cooler during the heat of the day.

Henry left me on my own while he went looking for a young man who had accepted the Lord. I couldn't talk to anyone, because no one spoke English. It was excruciatingly hot and I sat on a bench in a hut, feeling like I was going to melt. There was no movement to the air.

I finally went outside and stood under a tree that offered partial shade. At least I would catch any breath of air that came by.

Henry seemed to take for ever. Then, suddenly and without noticing a cloud in the sky, rain sprinkled down. Those cool drops felt so refreshing! The whole atmosphere seemed to change and I finally found the weather bearable. I began to wonder whether I could ever get used to all this tropical weather.

At long last, Henry reappeared and we continued visiting several other Maleku homes. They spoke to Henry in Spanish, and to each other in their native dialect, but I couldn't tell the difference. Both Spanish and Malekujaica were Greek to me.

We visited a large Hispanic family that lived nearby. When Henry had first met them, they'd been staunch Roman Catholics and hadn't appreciated the arrival of evangelicals. Henry had left them a Bible and the family's mother had read it. She had become convinced of the truth and later most of the family came to accept the Lord as their Saviour.

Towards evening, we went on to another Hispanic village and visited a believer who lived alone. The Spanish dwellers were usually a little less primitive in their way of life and this man had what I would have considered more of a normal dwelling—a small wooden hut with a boarded floor and leaf-covered kitchen beside it. The kitchen had a mud floor and vertical posts around the sides to keep the animals out. The boxlike stove was supported by four posts planted in the ground. The box would be filled with mud and rocks placed on the mud to support the pots, with the fire burning between the rocks. In contrast, I'd noticed that many of the Maleku people had done their cooking right on the ground.

Henry talked for a long time to this man. All the while, I wondered where this man kept his bed. What did he sleep on?

Finally, my curiosity was satisfied. When it came time to sleep, he got out a homemade broom made with a rounded stick and bushes tied to the stick with jungle vines. He started sweeping the floor. Then he got out a sheet that had obviously been repaired in a number of places, laying it on the floor where Henry and I were to rest.

What? I was to sleep on the bare floor with nothing but a sheet? Well, that was where we lay down, but I certainly didn't sleep. How could I? The hardwood floor didn't accommodate my hipbones very well.

I now understood what Henry had said to me in Ciudad Quesada: "Cheer up. Worse is yet to come."

Early in the morning, in partial daylight, we headed back to Guatuso to catch a flight back to Ciudad Quesada.

Suddenly, we heard a blood-curdling roar from a short distance into the woods. I was ready to run hard, but I glanced over at Henry and discovered that he was still carrying on at his usual stride.

"What was that?" I asked nervously.

"Oh, that was just a lion roaring," he explained in his usual calm voice.

Something didn't quite add up here. So after seeing that he couldn't fool me any further, he explained that there was a howling monkey that often made a sound like this, especially in the early morning hours.

We continued on to Guatuso and flew back to Ciudad Quesada, where we visited a number of homes, especially close to the airstrip. I believe the purpose of these visits were twofold: to be a witness for Jesus and to find out if there might be land available to purchase for a house Henry wanted to build when he returned.

As I watched the people wherever we went, I noticed that they listened to what Henry had to say. Some showed a keen interest. Others felt a bit uncomfortable and would respond by saying that they were Roman Catholics, excusing themselves from the issue. Still others said they were Catholic but admitted that, really, they weren't anything. Most people had been born to Roman Catholic parents and been baptized as infants. This observation burned in my mind as an opportunity for the gospel.

When we returned to the Mennonite centre in San José, it was a relief to be able to converse again in English.

However, that night I had a touch of Montezuma's revenge and spent a good part of the night in the bathroom. We were to catch our flight back home in the morning, but how could I go anywhere in the condition I was in? I could hardly last an hour without another trip to the bathroom.

We prayed about my dilemma—and when it got time to leave, I was doing a bit better. The Lord undertook for me and I had no more episodes, praise the Lord.

We arrived in Montreal without a hitch and had a boring drive back to Nova Scotia without any breakdowns at all.

But there is one more event I have to mention. I had what looked like mosquito bites on my ankles. In the succeeding days, those bites crept farther up my legs. I couldn't understand why, but Henry had mentioned something about grass lice.

After looking with a good light at the very centre of one raised spot, I noticed a very tiny spot that looked like speck of red chili powder. I removed it with the point of a knife and saw that it moved along the knife blade.

In the shower, I soaped up good and scratched the area where the bites were. Before long the lice were gone and only wished I had understood what to do sooner.

This was definitely a vacation to remember. More than that, I had a lot to think about in the days ahead.

PREPARING TO RETURN TO COSTA RICA
Summer 1968

My decision had been made to go to Costa Rica yet again, this time to assist in the missionary work for a longer period. I had informed my parents, but nothing much was said. I was just completing four years of training in electronics and now was making plans to set it all aside.

Although the Dockyard had planned to hire me full-time, I felt compelled to leave in order to pursue what I believed God was calling me to do. The personnel officer there even offered me a job if I later changed my mind and came back. I was pretty sure that wouldn't happen, but I thanked him for the offer in any case.

I realized it was necessary to pay all my debts prior to leaving for Costa Rica. I had a fairly new convertible which could only be paid by selling it, something I wasn't too anxious to do. Nevertheless, I put it on the market. I also sold various items I had acquired after working for four years at the Dockyard, including two sets of scuba gear.

Then things seemed to come to a standstill.

One day, while visiting my parents, Dad approached me abruptly and asked if I really knew what I was doing.

"You just spent four years in training. Now you are going to throw that all away?" Knowing that I didn't have a group supporting me, he added, "Where is your livelihood going to come from? You have to eat and you have to have money to buy clothes. Where is that going to come from?"

I needed to choose my words carefully. A verse of Scripture came clearly to my mind and I decided that this should be my answer: *"But seek ye first the kingdom of God, and his righteousness; and all these things shall be added unto you."*

Dad turned and walked away, shaking his head. He never said another word about it. I interpreted that to mean, in his mind, "If that's the way you believe, you're on your own. I'm not going to interfere."

It was getting close to the time when I was expected to meet up with Henry in Ontario. He and the family had gone ahead to prepare for the move to Costa Rica. I still hadn't found a buyer for my car, nor had I gotten any money back from some stock I'd sold since there was a postal strike holding up the mail. I needed that money to pay back a separate loan I had with the bank.

When Sunday arrived and I got ready to go to church, I decided in the spur of the moment to attend a different church than usual. The message at this church was about waiting on the Lord, and primarily rested on Isaiah 40:31: *"But they that wait upon the Lord shall renew their strength; they shall mount up with wings as eagles; they shall run, and not be weary; and they shall walk, and not faint."*

The pastor explained that there were three types of conditions to our walk with God. One is when things happen fast and we fly through our experiences. This is the illustration of mounting up with wings as eagles. There are other times when things don't happen quite as fast but strength is needed so we don't become weary and tire out. Then there are times when things move very slowly. He compared this to walking in a desert where there is very little change of scenery, and maybe it's unbearably hot—in other words, *"they shall walk, and not faint."*

Suddenly, it clicked. I was in the middle of making preparations for my move to Costa Rica and found myself reflecting on the first part of this verse: *"But they that wait upon the Lord shall renew their strength."*

"There's my problem," I concluded to myself. "I'm not waiting on the Lord. So I'll stop worrying about things not working out. If they don't work out, then it means God doesn't want me to go to Costa Rica. It would be better to tell everyone I made a mistake than go to Costa Rica and not be where God wants me to be."

In that moment, the burden of concern left me.

The next morning, a cheque arrived in the mail from the cancelled stock, granting me a total of $236.18. I was so surprised at the amount because the value of the stock had been steadily falling since the postal strike had begun.

On Tuesday morning, a bill came for the balance due on my small loan. It added up to $236.10—only eight cents less than the stock payout!

On Wednesday, a guy I knew offered to buy my car and suggested that I keep the car until I was actually ready to depart. He knew I would need a form of transportation while preparing to leave.

This was more than I could have asked for, and it meant I had no further obstacles in the way of leaving for Costa Rica. I was completely satisfied that God was leading me to the mission field.

If that weren't enough, I had one more surprise. The day before the train was to take me to Ontario, I went to my parents' home for a final visit. My mother informed me that my cousin and her husband were leaving the next day for Ontario and from there were flying to Japan to serve as missionaries!

I called my cousin and they offered for me to travel with them, as they had lots of room in their vehicle. What were the chances of their plans coinciding exactly with mine? I much preferred to travel by car than by train!

Lord, I didn't need that, I mused, *but you have put the frosting on the cake for me. Thank you.*

Six

COSTA RICA, HERE WE COME
Fall 1968

As soon as my cousin and her husband arrived to pick me up, we were off to Ontario. We enjoyed each other's company as we travelled and the conversations seemed to make the time fly by. Their destination was Ottawa, whereas mine was Port Rowan, so we parted ways and I continued my journey by bus.

It was harvest time in Ontario and the Teigrobs used this opportunity to keep the family busy. Tomato-picking was in full swing, and we were told that this was a job for someone with a strong back and a weak mind. I guessed they meant that a person didn't have to be very smart to figure out how to pick tomatoes, but it sure didn't take long before we found out whether we had strong backs.

At the same time, Henry steadily prepared to travel south. The Teigrob family was large, as there were ten of them, varying in age from toddler to the early teens. As the tagalong, I became number eleven. To affordably transport the family, Henry had purchased an old-school bus and was renovating it for the trip. Henry's plan was to sell it to a Costa Rican bus company when we arrived there.

To save fuel, he fastened a ball hitch on the back of the bus to tow his VW van.

By the time we were finally ready to leave, we had become quite the talk of the town. Even some media people showed up with cameras. Henry didn't want to draw too much attention, though, so we didn't delay long in getting on the road.

The seats inside the bus had been rearranged and there was a living area up front with a table for serving meals and playing games as we travelled the long journey. Being a bit like a camper, the children had some liberty to move around; as you can imagine, they were very excited about travelling this way. If they got tired, they could lay on their beds whenever they wanted.

As we travelled, the family often sang songs, many of which they knew by heart. Many were new to me, but a couple in particular were so often repeated that they became favourites of mine: "My Lord Knows the Way Through the Wilderness" and "A Shelter in the Time of Storm."

We faced plenty of obstacles along the way, but God opened the way for us. All we have to do is to wait for Him. We don't have to carry that concern on our shoulders.

As the first night fell, one by one the children got tired and laid down in their beds. Eventually, Anne also retired. Soon only Henry and I remained awake, although I was struggling with drowsiness. I figured I should stay awake to ensure that Henry didn't fall asleep at the wheel. I decided to stand and hold on to a vertical post for balance so as to keep alert. These were the days before I knew what coffee would do for me.

Suddenly, my knees buckled and I had to grab hold of the post to avoid falling. After this happened a few times, I realized that I was the greater liability; Henry seemed quite wide awake as he drove through the evening hours. So I went to the back of the bus and laid down as well.

Within a few days, we arrived at the Mexican border. The customs officials refused to allow us into the country until we paid a "bond" to guarantee that we wouldn't be selling the bus in Mexico. The term "bond" seemed a bit strange, since we were told that the money wouldn't be returned to us.

While we were delayed, we met up with another missionary who was working in Durango, Mexico. Being very familiar with Mexican food, she offered to order a meal for everyone. She ordered a dish that had a mild amount of chili, and another dish with more chili in it. I chose the mild version, thinking I could graduate to the hotter one later on. The carrots and other vegetables didn't appear to be any different than what I was used to, but I soon realized that I wouldn't be touching the hotter stuff. Indeed, the mild dish had more takers than the hot one.

We finally got on our way and were happy to put the border behind us. But then, not far out on the road, we came to a checkpoint. We didn't know if these officials would go through all our belongings again. Fortunately, after checking our papers, they sent us on our way.

About an hour later, though, we came to yet another checkpoint. Again they rechecked all the paperwork and finally allowed us to continue.

It took four days of travel to get across Mexico. There were no four-lane highways as in the United States. The roads were rather narrow and, in some places, had lots of traffic. The towns and cities were often a chore to find our way through, for there were very few signs to direct us. Many times we found the signs affixed to the walls of corner buildings.

When Henry needed to ask for directions, he would ask two different people. If the directions they gave did not correspond, he would ask another person until he had two that matched. On two occasions, the people he asked jumped into their vehicles and escorted us to the other side of the town or city, not wanting us to get lost.

At last we reached the border with Guatemala. We weren't anticipating any difficulty in leaving Mexico, but the inspecting officer said that we were missing a certain paper showing that our bond had been paid. Although Henry pointed to a paper that stated exactly that fact, they insisted that our paperwork wasn't acceptable. We would have to wait until the officials received verification from our port of entry—

and it would take time. It was obvious that these officials were looking for a handout more than anything else.

This took place on a Friday afternoon.

Henry kept checking with the officials. Whenever there was a shift change, he would check to see if the new arrivals would let us go. That didn't happen. We waited that night, all the next day, and on into Sunday.

We were self-sufficient in our bus, except that we needed to use the washrooms in the immigration building. We managed all right, although the parked bus got warm and there wasn't much air movement.

Finally, on Sunday afternoon, a shift came on that had some compassion on us and let us leave the country. We felt like singing again "The Lord Knows the Way Through the Wilderness."

We crossed over into Guatemala and endeavoured to get permission to travel through this much smaller country. They required an escort soldier to travel with us to the southern border, and we had to pay his expenses plus his fare by bus back to the northern border afterward. It was, to say the least, awkward to accommodate a stranger on board, but we did what we had to do.

This was one of two countries that required us to take along an escort. One advantage of having an escort was that we never had problems finding our way through towns and cities.

A major hurdle we faced had to do with money-changing. Were we getting a fair exchange? If you didn't know the going rate ahead of time, you were likely to get taken to the cleaners, as we say in Canada. And how much money would we need? If we changed more than we needed, we would lose on the exchange again when we converted it back to American dollars. But if we didn't have enough, we could run into trouble.

We came across vendors at many different places along the highway. We avoided the homemade drinks and cooked pastries they sold, though, to avoid picking up a parasite or microorganism. However, we could trust the sealed drinks and intact fruits. Without air-conditioning, we consumed plenty of liquids to keep us hydrated.

And we certainly didn't want to take any risks that might result in illness along the way.

We travelled through El Salvador into Honduras and on to Nicaragua. It didn't take long to travel through these countries, being small, but it would have been a much more enjoyable journey were it not for the frequent border crossings. Border crossings were always a matter of high concern, and they were definitely a matter of prayer.

Once we finally arrived in Costa Rica, it was another eight hours of travel to get to Alajuela, a town near San José. Henry knew some people there who had a fair-sized yard where we could park the bus.

During the trip, the children talked about a fruit they claimed to be the best they had ever eaten. They whet my appetite for a fruit that I had heretofore been deprived of the privilege of tasting.

Shortly after arriving in Alajuela, the children disappeared somewhere. I went looking for them and found them up a tree.

"What are you doing?" I asked.

"We're eating guayabas," one of them replied.

My mouth was watering. "Oh. Can I try one?"

"Sure."

I took one bite, then threw it on the ground and spit out what had been in my mouth. "It's full of maggots!"

The next one they gave me was the same. Then they told me that the green ones were best, because they never had any maggots in them. Well, a green one didn't taste at all appetizing.

Wow, I thought. *What a letdown!*

After living in the country for some time, I did develop at least a tolerance for these guayabas. But I can't say I ever craved them, like my fellow travellers.

I found out much later that the fruit is high in vitamin A and C. So if you could forget about the maggots, they were a great choice while in Costa Rica.

Guayabas can be white or pink inside.

Seven

GOD'S LEADING TO THE MALEKU
1958

After arriving in Costa Rica, we had to find a temporary place to live in Ciudad Quesada. I found a Spanish home where I could board for the next few months. Henry purchased a piece of land right beside the airstrip to build a house, because he had a vision of eventually buying an airplane to help the family travel back and forth to Guatuso, as opposed to taking the family to live in the lowlands again.

To put this in perspective, allow me to retrace Henry and Anne's first mission trip to Costa Rica approximately ten years earlier.

They had received boot training with New Tribes Mission, now called Ethnos360. They had felt the Lord leading them in a pioneer work with an unreached group in Panama. Highways there had been closed due to the weather at the time, however, so they had decided to remain in Costa Rica and attend a linguistics institute to become more fluent in the language before they travelled farther.

While in Costa Rica, a need arose for them to fill in for some missionaries who wanted to go back to the United States on furlough. They would be working with a native group called the Bribri who live on the southern extremity of the country, in a place called Talamanca on the border with Panama.

During their stay in Talamanca, Henry heard about a group of natives called Maleku living in the north of the country, a group who had not heard the gospel and weren't being reached by any evangelicals. So after the missionaries returned from furlough, Henry and family moved to Guatuso, which was within walking distance of the people he sought to reach.

The question sometimes comes up as to whether these people would have been better off, and happier, if they had been left to themselves. I can't speak of specifics for every case, but I can argue the point when it comes to the Maleku. If anyone feels that way, I would ask them to continue reading and then judge for themselves.

These people had a harsh history and it is estimated that about ninety percent of their population had died throughout the 1900s. One village had suffered so many deaths that it was called "The Death," and the name remains. One man told me that he had run away from that village as a boy to save his own life. Every native person who remained there eventually died and now only Hispanics remain.

Even in the latter half of the century, a very low percentage of children made it past two years of age. One man I knew of was the only member of his eleven-person family to make it to adulthood.

One might think that a people accustomed to so much death wouldn't have such raw feelings about death, but I beg to differ. I witnessed the death of a two-year-old. The mother, family, and neighbours wailed over the loss for weeks. The mother continued wailing for two months and she could be heard as soon as a person entered the village.

Tuberculosis claimed the lives of many and the disease still ran rampant while Henry and I worked there. Malaria, which reoccurs later in life when a person's immunity is low, was quite common and both Henry and one of his sons contracted it. There were also parasitical infections of many types that were just as common as a cold. The source of drinking water was the river, and it often wasn't boiled before it was consumed.

I must say that I didn't know how bad the situation was for these people before I went to Costa Rica, or I might have had a harder time convincing myself that God was leading me there. Henry knew, of course. When he told me the worst was yet to come, I would ask, "How much worse?" He never offered to say.

These people had a great physical need *and* a great spiritual need. Natural man doesn't recognize that sin separates us from God, who is our source of help in every kind of need.

However, these people weren't ready to confide in a stranger's help, either physical or spiritual. The Maleku had their own beliefs, as do seemingly every people group the world over. How do you, as a stranger, convince someone to believe in a different God that, you say, revealed himself in a very special way through another group of people?

Rather than put the cart before the horse, so to speak, our actions must first speak louder than our words. You know they have a desperate physical need. Meeting that need may open the door a little for them to listen, but they have a history of being mistreated by strangers. You may have a genuine concern for them, but they don't know that. You have to win their trust and that takes a painstakingly long time.

Henry had a plan of action. After he won these people's friendship, he talked them into setting apart some land to build an airstrip which would be used to fly people out who needed medical help. After getting their cooperation in all the hard work building the runway, it was another matter to convince them to go with him in his small plane to the hospital when they needed care.

A man named Antonio told me his testimony years later. He had possibly been the first person with a serious medical need who Henry tried to get to come with him in his plane to the hospital in Ciudad Quesada. He'd developed a huge swelling on the side of his head. He would have rather stayed home and died than go with Henry, even though he wouldn't have had to pay any expenses.

Finally, Henry gave him until noon the next day to make up his mind.

It was an answer to prayer that when Henry arrived the next day with his little yellow, canvas-covered plane, Antonio had changed his mind and decided to go. Henry prayed for the trip and the man's medical needs before they got aboard. Flying in an airplane was a new and a bit frightening experience for this young lad, but he managed.

Antonio arrived at the hospital and had to see the doctor on his own. The doctor didn't show much concern and told him that nothing could be done for him.

The young man left the doctor's office and went back out to see Henry in the waiting room. It just so happened that a visiting doctor from the U.S. was sitting there. When he noticed Antonio and the swelling, he came over to talk. Antonio told this doctor that they were sending him home—and so the American doctor asked to examine him.

It turned out that there was a medication that would help him. To make a long story short, the medication did work and this young man was forever grateful.

God answered prayer in changing Antonio's mind, then in putting in place the right doctor, in the right place at the right time. Seeing God work goes a long way towards opening doors for the truth.

This was a small beginning. Over time, Henry conducted more medical airlifts and many visits. But there were also many setbacks and tears. As Psalm 126:6 tells us, *"He that goes forth weeping, bearing the seed for sowing, shall come home with shouts of joy, bringing his sheaves with him"* (RSV).

Henry and Anne sacrificed a lot, living in the lowland in the tropical heat with their large family, and they eventually made a decision to return to Canada. Whether they had planned to return again to Costa Rica, I don't know, but they did come home.

After spending some time with family and friends in Ontario, they decided to move to Nova Scotia and see what the Lord had for them there. That is, of course, how I came to make my acquaintance with them—and my story would have been totally different if they hadn't made that move.

Eight

EARLY DAYS IN COSTA RICA
1968–1970

After we were partly settled in Ciudad Quesada, we had to endure numerous trips to the capital to get our paperwork ready in order to stay in the country. We also had to get our vehicles insured and licensed.

Trying to sort out these legal matters was frustrating. Instead of going to one office building to get an item taken care of, we would have to make many stops. We'd go to one place and wait in line for a good while, only to have the attendant stamp our paper, give us another paper, and send us somewhere else across the city. We often took a taxi to speed things up, but, I think, for little avail. When we'd get there, we would just have to wait in line again—then, of course, get our paper stamped and given another to be taken elsewhere.

After several similar experiences, we began to wonder if we were being given the runaround. Patience is a virtue, we would remind ourselves, but were we actually accomplishing anything? Sometimes the officials would tell us to come back the next day or the next week. We never knew when we came back whether the runaround was over.

However, God knows the way through the wilderness and all we have to do is follow.

Walking the streets of the centre of San José was often a challenge. The sidewalks were usually very wide, as they needed to be to accommodate large crowds of people. It was very difficult to walk side by side, as we would normally prefer. We made far better progress by proceeding in single file. It often happened that the lead person would either stop or step aside to avoid bumping into someone, and the interruption would leave a gap—a gap which would be quickly filled by some stranger before it was possible for the trailing person to catch up. It would start with one stranger, then grow to two or three or four.

This once happened to me as I tried to follow Henry. He was kind of tall, so at least I could see his head bobbing above the shorter nationals.

But then he was suddenly gone.

I came to a street crossing, unable to find him, and asked myself, *Did he go straight? Did he turn to the left or the right? Did he stop into a store somewhere?* My dilemma was that I hardly knew a word of Spanish and didn't know the way back. If I ventured to look for him, his chances of finding me would be extremely slim. And if I went looking for someone who spoke English, I would expose myself to a great vulnerability; I had heard of too many people who had been taken advantage of by strangers pretending to offer help.

So I stood with my back to the wall and waited, trying to look as at ease as possible, as though I were just taking in the sunshine.

Henry apparently had entered a store. After purchasing what he had gone for, he came out and looked for me.

"What happened to you?" he asked, as though getting lost had somehow been my fault.

When our time ran out for the day and it wasn't possible to complete any more errands, he sometimes asked if I thought it might be a good idea to go somewhere for some apple pie and ice cream before heading back. I never disagreed, and it became our usual practice every time we came to the city for business.

My immediate necessities were twofold: to learn Spanish and to study the Bible. I had a parallel English-Spanish Bible and I spent many hours translating back and forth between them. However, to better learn the language and to understand it when spoken, I chose to board in a Spanish home. That may seem like a hard situation to put oneself in, but it was the best situation for me. If I had been with people who spoke English, my progress would have been slower; it would have been easier for me to cop out.

Conversing was always a struggle, but the people around me were generally very helpful and wanted to help me learn. They had a great many laughs at my mistakes, though, some of which they no doubt still remember.

In the house where I boarded, I often tried to describe something and got stuck on a word I didn't know. The woman of the house, the wife of the doctor who owned it, seemed to have a tremendous gift for guessing the word I meant, enabling me to continue with what I was trying to say.

By two and a half months, I had broken the ice and could converse, after a fashion, with most people. If I didn't know a word, I could usually at least describe what I meant. However, it took two years before I reached a level where I felt at ease to witness to people without stumbling or mispronouncing words.

Later, I rented a whole house for $11 per month. This may seem outrageous, but you must understand the cost of living in Costa Rica at the time. Every time I came home at night, I went through a certain ritual. As I entered, I would take off one shoe, leave the lights off, and proceed with flashlight and shoe in hand. I would start killing cockroaches on the walls. This would go on until there was not a cockroach to be seen. Then I would turn on the lights and sweep up the dead cockroaches.

This was another one those chores in Costa Rica that Henry had failed to mention.

I came to know about another interesting insect. On one occasion, I bought one pound of sugar, along with other groceries. Foods were very reasonably priced and often I could live on five dollars a week. That is, if I didn't splurge. Anyway, the store workers had placed the sugar in a brand-new brown paper bag.

When I got home that day, I dropped the bag of sugar onto the table in the centre of the room. Since it was night, I decided not to put the sugar away in a plastic container until morning.

First thing in the morning, I got up and prepared to sweeten my coffee. But when I looked in the bag, the sugar was completely covered with tiny sugar ants! How had they found it so quickly?

With the legs of the table so far from the edge of the table, it was amazing that they, from the underside, knew to orient themselves to the perimeter before coming up on top and heading for the sugar bag.

I got rid of most of these ants, along with the top layer of sugar. After sweetening my coffee, I sealed the rest in a tight container.

The language barrier was one of two great challenges that had concerned me most before I came to Costa Rica. Only by being convinced that God had sent me was I able to face them.

I had studied French throughout school yet still couldn't catch what people said when they spoke in French. I wondered if I would ever be able to learn a second language.

The second challenge was to grow accustomed to the hot climate. In the heat of a Canadian summer growing up on the farm, I had often needed to unload loose hay from the trailer or wagon into the mows of the barn to store it up for the cows in winter. A large fork device had been connected to a heavy rope, carrying the hay up into the mows and dropping it in a pile. The job I'd most dreaded was to spread the hay from the pile to the extremities of the mow.

The heat of the hay in a mow, without any breeze, had been almost too much for me. How would I ever get used to the heat of the tropics?

As time went on, I saw both of these mountains moved out of the way.

In the beginning, I helped the Teigrobs build their house. Then, since it was harvest time for coffee, we all took on the job of harvesting, except for Anne and their youngest son, James. This was a way for us to put ourselves on the level of the people around us, even though the amount of money we could earn after a hard day's work under the heat of the sun or the chill of falling rain was probably less than we could have earned in fifteen minutes of work in Canada.

EIGHT: EARLY DAYS IN COSTA RICA

Most of the people were Roman Catholics and foreigners, like in most countries, weren't readily treated as equals. Costa Ricans are generally well known for their hospitality, but that only goes so far. As I walked the streets of Ciudad Quesada, local children would peer out of the doors and windows and shout "Macho!" or "Gringo!" Neither of which is very glamorous. Over time, I kind of wished they would shake the habit.

There were no permanent roads in Guatuso and the only means of access was by plane, foot, horseback, or, if you had the time, oxcart. It was expensive to transport cargo by plane, so only essential cargo and people with urgent needs travelled that way.

Living on the mountainous terrain around Ciudad Quesada, we often had rainy spells, called *temporales* that lasted several days in a row. If the cloud and fog lifted a bit, the pilots would attempt to get some flights in. Often they couldn't make it back, though, because the clouds had lowered again. Since the terrain dropped abruptly to almost sea level, the pilots could usually make it back to the foot of the mountain range where they could land on an emergency landing strip.

Henry often helped around the airport and flew the odd flight when needed. On one particular occasion, inclement weather set in. There was a scheduled flight to a fair-sized farm which produced milk, but the pilot was only able to land at the foot of the mountain.

The milk carried on this plane needed to be transported by road to Ciudad Quesada, and the owner of the flying company asked Henry if he would do this. So Henry, three of his boys, and I jumped into his trusty VW van and headed down the mountain road to pick up six large cans of milk. Just before we arrived at the airstrip, though, we came to a river that didn't have a bridge crossing it—and the water was high. How high, we didn't really know.

Dwight, the second youngest boy, was afraid that his father would attempt to cross the river and he had it in his mind that we wouldn't make it across.

"Daddy, don't go," Dwight said, already in tears. "Don't go…"

He knew his dad rather well, but not enough to best know how to stop him. I think that if he had said, "Go ahead, Daddy, you can do it," Henry might have backed down. But Henry was never one to back away from adversity, and Dwight's telling him not to go, I believe, only prodded him on.

We got close to halfway across the river when the van started to float downstream. The motor gurgled and then quit.

Fortunately, the river got shallower a little way's down from our initial point of crossing and so the van came to a stop while water seeped in. At this point, poor Dwight broke down crying.

"I told you, Daddy… I told you not to go."

There we sat, or at least Henry and I did, while the boys stood in the back of the van, up to their waists in water.

Eventually a large diesel tractor came by and offered to pull us out. We got out and wadded onto the riverbank as they hooked a chain to the bumper. The water made it difficult to connect the chain elsewhere.

The van started to emerge, but the water still trapped inside the vehicle made it very heavy. Suddenly, the entire bumper buckled in half and ripped off.

Anyway, now the driver of the tractor could better see where to secure the chain. He ended up towing us back to a sugarcane processing plant so we could get in out of the spitting rain and work on drying out the motor to hopefully get it going again.

In the meantime, the tractor driver went out with a trailer to fetch the milk cans from across the river.

Finally, after much effort, we got the motor dry enough so the vehicle would start, although it was only firing on two of four cylinders.

We put the milk cans in the van and headed up the mountain. By the time we got to the steeper part of the climb, we were at least firing on three cylinders, otherwise I know we wouldn't have made it up.

It wasn't until we were almost to the top before all four cylinders were doing their part.

Well, that was a rather memorable event with the van! But it was certainly not the last. We had a bit of an issue with the transmission on this trusty old machine. From time to time, the transmission would slip out of gear.

EIGHT: EARLY DAYS IN COSTA RICA

Henry decided that the van needed to be fixed. Well, he didn't want to pay a fortune, so to cut costs we pulled the engine and transmission out. Since neither of us had taken apart a transmission before, Henry took it to a mechanic who claimed to have done several of these jobs before.

This mechanic attempted to take the cover off the gear box but he couldn't lift it free. He pried and hammered for some time, but when lunch came he gave up to go eat. While he was away, Henry became convinced that the man had never taken one of these apart before. He went down the street to talk to another mechanic who he believed had more knowledge about the problem at hand.

When the first guy came back from his lunch, Henry told him that we were going to take the transmission to another mechanic. The guy just nodded his head and never said a word.

The second mechanic told us that we had to first remove the axials, exposing four more bolts that would allow the transmission to come apart.

After the transmission was repaired, we brought it back to the van and installed it. However, when we tried to start the vehicle, nothing happened. We towed it up and down several streets, to no avail.

Henry tried it again with the key and away it went. But when he put the transmission into gear, the van backed up. He tried running the van in second and third, and it backed up each time. But when he tried putting it in reverse, the van moved forward.

It turned out the mechanic had reinstalled the axials backwards. The motor and transmission would have to be removed and the axials reversed and then reassembled.

Were our problems over? No. Even after the transmission was fixed, it kept slipping out of a different gear. Eventually we found out that adjusting this transmission requires one to remove the existing casing and install a special casing with holes in the sides to allow access. Then the casings can be exchanged and everything put back together again.

The transmission had to be sent to San José to get this done. What it all cost, Henry never told me, and I didn't feel like asking him.

Nine

BAPTISM

More than one issue played itself out after I met the Teigrobs. On that first occasion when Henry and I talked together at my grandparents' home, he questioned me about baptism. I assured him that, as far as I was concerned, I had been baptized at six years of age. Even though the Scriptures say that *"he who believes and is baptized will be saved"* (Mark 15:16, RSV), it could just as easily have said "he who is baptized and believes will be saved." I couldn't see any strength to the argument.

However, I wasn't bull-headed about it and I agreed to carefully study any portion of Scripture that dealt with baptism.

"Unless I see convincing scripture that I needed to believe before I was baptized, then I would remain the way I am," I said.

I stuck to my promise over the next months. In my studies, I was a bit surprised about the reason Jesus gave for his water baptism. In Matthew 3:15, his answer to John the Baptist was to *"fulfil all righteousness."* He was already righteous and had reason to go through with the baptism, so how much more reason did I have, as a sinner? But the order of events so far, in my mind, wasn't an issue.

Eventually, I came across 1 Peter 3:21, which says, *"The like figure whereunto even baptism doth also now save us (not the putting away of the filth of the flesh, but the answer of a good conscience toward God,) by the resurrection of Jesus Christ..."*

Wow! That hit me like a ton of bricks. At six years of age, I'd had no conscience toward God at all, so I hadn't been answering to a good conscience toward him. This invalided my childhood baptism. Baptism is a testimony of the faith a person has in Jesus and testifies that a person believes that Jesus died, was buried in a tomb, and rose again. This realization shook me.

Next question: where was I going to get baptized? The church I attended didn't baptize adults, so I checked out a Baptist church. The pastor there wanted me to attend a number of classes first, so that I could be baptized and become a member of the church. I had a problem with that, since I believed that joining a church was one thing and identifying with Christ quite another.

I understood very clearly at this point what the Bible said about baptism and I believed that I was ready to be baptized. I didn't want to join a church. Besides, I was leaving very shortly for Costa Rica and didn't have time to attend classes.

I later talked to Henry about this and he told me that his church would probably have said the same thing. He assured me that I could get baptized in Costa Rica, so that settled the issue for the time being.

After being in Costa Rica for a short while, Henry and I paid a visit to the Maleku people. In the evening, the believers had planned to celebrate the Lord's supper. I expected to participate in the Lord's supper, as I had done for many years. When the plate was about to be passed around, though, Henry told me that I couldn't participate because I wasn't baptized.

This took me totally by surprise. Here I had come all the way from Canada to represent Christ, but now I somehow didn't qualify to even share the Lord's supper? That hit me very hard. I didn't say anything at the time because my Spanish was very limited and it wouldn't have been convenient to have a discussion right then. My thinking was that if this was how Henry felt, he should have arranged for me to be baptized before it came time to celebrate the Lord's supper. He had known for some time that I desired to be baptized. If I had done it by now, nothing would have hindered my participation.

After some time had passed and I had become much more fluent in Spanish, I went out exploring around the city of Quesada. It was a Sunday morning and I heard singing coming from one of the homes I passed. As I got closer, I recognized that they were singing Christian songs.

I ventured into the house to join them and I was soon able to discern that they were seemingly an evangelical group. After the service, I talked with the pastor about the church and inquired about their doctrinal beliefs. I was a bit surprised when the pastor asked whether I had been baptized.

"I'm not," I had to tell him.

"Why?"

"Because I haven't had the opportunity."

"Do you understand what the Bible says about baptism?"

"Yes," I said. "I believe I know quite well what the Bible says about baptism."

That didn't satisfy him. He sat me down at a table and asked a number of doctrinal questions to see if I really did understand baptism.

Afterward, he finally turned to the congregation who were still hanging around and asked, "Does anyone see any reason why we can't go right now to the river and baptize this man?"

"No," they answered in unison.

"Then let's go to the river."

The whole congregation trudged down a narrow pathway to the river. I can't say I had come prepared with a change of clothes, but at least it was a pleasantly warm day so my clothes wouldn't take long to dry.

It was a memorable day and so tremendously satisfying to have completed this commandment of God.

When I got back to Henry and Anne's place and told them what had transpired, they were not at all pleased. They said that I should have informed them first. However, I had waited too long already. We can't always act in unison and there are times when we have to act as individuals to be faithful to God.

Henry was quite sceptical about this group. The next Sunday, he went with me to the service. After getting to know their doctrine more specifically, he not only was quite impressed but he and the rest of the family joined them for many services after that.

Ten

THE MALEKU MINISTRY
1968, 1974

Our primary focus of ministry was with the Maleku, although we were trying to leave an impact for the gospel wherever we went. At first I spent more time in Ciudad Quesada than in the palenques, but every week or two we flew in to visit, especially while I was learning the language.

Later, I would stay with the people for a week, then two weeks, and eventually a month at a time. I noticed that every time I came to the lowlands from the higher altitude, I found the climate quite uncomfortable for the first three days; after that, it wasn't nearly as difficult to endure. I got used to sleeping on floors or on benches and eating what the people ate.

If I had been married at this time, I wouldn't have been able to spend nearly as much time with these people.

I thought of Matthew 8:20 where Jesus says, *"Foxes have holes, and birds of the air have nests, but the Son of Man has nowhere to lay his head."* He didn't have a place of his own.

Over time it seemed a bit degrading to always be sleeping in people's corridors, which were really half-outdoor. Nevertheless, some people did offer me places to sleep inside.

As I relied totally on people's provision, I thought of the scripture in Luke 10:7: *"And in the same house remain, eating and drinking such things as they give: for the labourer is worthy of his hire. Go not from house to house."*

In each village I visited, I stayed where I was first invited. I felt a bit like a vagabond but looked for every chance to help the people any way I could. The list of things I could help them with seemed endless. I hunted and fished with them, even going on an eight-day journey to Caña Negro to catch turtles. I came to feel safer with them in the jungle than I would ever have felt on my own, even with all the experience I had.

In fact, the more familiar I became with the dangers of the jungle, the more I relied on them to watch out for me. On one occasion, while hunting deep in the jungle with a young man named Elíjio. I was taking the lead down a narrow trail when I came to a large tree trunk that lay across the path. My plan was to put my hand on it and flip my legs up over it. Just as I was about to put my hand down, I felt a sudden slap on my shoulder. I quickly realized it was Elíjio.

"What?" I asked, feeling a little irritated.

"Did you see where you were going to put your hand?"

I turned back to look at the log and noticed a grey snake curled in a circle, inches from where I was about to place my hand on the tree trunk. The snake was ready to strike. Had it bit me, I might never have made it out of the jungle.

That young man quite likely saved my life. I've often thought about how he reacted to me. He never shouted anything, just reacted in a split second and stopped me. I was very surprised that he had seen from behind what I hadn't.

Over time, I did win the appreciation and trust of the Maleku. To give an illustration, I will relate an incident that occurred on a jungle trail.

First, however, you need to understand something about Spanish culture. When you meet up with someone, they always say hello and shake your hand. Adults make sure that even the younger generation participates in this way.

On the trail one day, Elíjio and myself met up with a person he knew but I didn't. The stranger never said hello to me or shook my hand. He started talking straightaway and continued for some time. And instead of saying hello to me and asking who I was, he nodded in my direction and asked Elíjio who I was.

Elíjio, sensing this man's rudeness towards me, didn't give him the satisfaction of the expected answer.

"Oh, he is one of us," Elíjio said.

Well, I looked nothing like these people physically. The guy seemed to realize his own rudeness and quickly went on his way.

It felt so good to be accepted to the point of being defended like that.

Up to this point, we hadn't visited the palenque of Tonjibe, as Henry had told me they weren't very open to the gospel. I had a real burden to reach Tonjibe, though, so I began to pray about it. I also inquired among those who listened to the gospel from the other villages if they knew anyone who might be interested in the gospel from Tonjibe.

Armed with four names, I visited the village for the first time. Two of the names were brothers and they invited me to their home. I eventually started meetings in their village, and they even invited me to stay with them at nights. The parents gave me a spot on the floor between the brothers, usually with a shirt and a pair of pants laid out for a bedsheet. They afforded me the luxury of sleeping inside instead of a wooden bench out in the corridor.

When we were about to lie down, one of the boys would light three candles, one near to each of us. One of them would then start with a question and I would look up the answer in my Bible as they followed along in theirs. Then the other would fire a question. This would continue until all three candles had burnt out and they were satisfied they had received enough answers. Then we would drop off to sleep.

The morning would start early. I would awake around 5:00 a.m., but this was late for the villagers who always got up at 4:00 a.m. and ventured down a steep, hundred-foot riverbank to wash. By five o'clock, they would have already returned and gotten breakfast ready.

The mother of the family would peek in the room to see if I was awake. If she saw that I was waking up, she would go out to her leaf-roofed cooking place and dish out rice and beans onto a plate. She'd pour black sugared coffee into a cup and put everything on the table.

"Hay está su café," she'd say, meaning "There is your breakfast."

Then she would dish out food for the two boys, the oldest of the children still living in the home. My plate would be plenty full, but theirs would be twice as high. They took no time at all devouring their food and even went back for equal refills. That, too, would be gone before I'd gotten halfway through my portion.

After breakfast, they would jump up and say goodbye before hurrying off to work.

The people had one growing season per year. They would cut down the jungle where they planned to plant towards the end of the rainy season, usually between December and March, then let the weather dry out the fallen trees and brush. Just before the rains started again in late May or early June, they would set it on fire to leave the land clear for planting—except for the big tree trunks, which they would step over and plant in between.

After they harvested their crops, whether it be corn, rice, or beans, they would spread it out on a tarp or something on the ground to dry in the sun. When they were dry enough, they were gathered up in bags to be kept throughout the year. They often ran out of some of these products before the next crop could be harvested and didn't have the money to buy more.

Since I ate what they ate, if they had rice without beans, I had rice without beans. If they had beans without rice, I had beans without rice. I only had meat when they'd hunted some animal or killed a chicken or pig. I sometimes went without meat for a couple of weeks at a time.

Realizing that sometimes my diet wasn't the best, I prayed and asked God what I should do about it. His answer was to take advantage of the guayabas that grew wild in the pasture lands between the palenques. I disciplined myself to eat one fruit each time I passed under those trees even if I didn't really want one. I didn't know until years later that they were high in vitamin A and C.

Sometimes I received more variety when Spanish farmers asked me to come to their place to work on something. I trusted God completely for my food. If I was travelling during a meal and wasn't offered food before I left, I might get to the next village after meal. In that case, I wouldn't eat until the next mealtime.

On one occasion, I was given a meal that included meat on a large bone. After I finished eating and left the table, the neighbour Pedro came over and walked straight to the table, picked up the bone, and started chewing on it. Other members of the family smirked and laughed.

"The problem is that hermano Dónal doesn't know how to eat bones," said the woman of the house where I stayed in this village. Dónal, of course, was me.

Of course I knew what she meant but I responded, "That is exactly right."

Everybody laughed heartedly.

Leonel's mother came to live with her son after her husband had died. She would ask me for the time; then, before I could answer, she would look up into the sky and say what time she thought it was.

One day, she told me why she had become a Christian. After drinking one night, not an uncommon activity for the natives, she had done something foolish. It had been raining a lot and the river was high. She'd gone out in bare feet to get water from the river at night without a light—and gotten bit by a snake. This had scared her a lot, because the Maleku believe that if you die of a snakebite, the devil has taken you away. God spared her and she had turned her life over to the Lord.

She was among the first of the older generation to trust Christ as her Saviour.

She had raised her grandson, and this two-year-old boy always sat on my lap during for the services, and many times with a bare bottom. He never squirmed a bit and just observed what was going on. He never opened his mouth, even when we sang.

When I would get up to deliver the message, his grandmother would take him and lay him down to sleep. Sometime later, while sitting on a blanket by himself with his grandmother working nearby, he would begin to sing some of the lyrics of a song he had picked up.

One day I arrived at Tonjibe late in the afternoon. As I approached a hut, I noticed a woman sitting in her corridor with a fair-sized boy on her lap. The woman looked very sad.

As I got closer, I saw that the boy had a badly swollen foot with a red-coloured infection that appeared to be advancing toward the ankle. The woman pulled up his pantleg to reveal more swelling halfway between the ankle and the knee. She proceeded to show me yet another area of swelling at the groin.

My heart sank. It was the rainy season and the nearest place to get penicillin would require walking two or three hours each way. I didn't have the physical strength to do it.

"Your son is very ill," I said to the woman.

She nodded her head up and down.

"Do you believe that God can heal your son?"

Again, she nodded.

"Excuse me," I said. "I will come right back."

I went looking for all the villagers who had showed interest in the gospel. I told them that I wanted them to join me in prayer for this ill boy, for he could be dead by morning unless God performed a miracle.

They seemed to understand the seriousness of the situation.

When we got back to the woman's house, I asked if she had any oil or lard, which I explained represented the Holy Spirit.

We then gathered around and I explained that we were going to pray for the boy, since God alone heals. The woman nodded.

I anointed the boy with whatever it was they had given me in place of oil. I led in prayer, and afterward I left to prepare for the evening service.

We prayed again during the service, mentioning to the congregation that the boy was seriously ill.

After the service, I quickly returned to the house where I always stayed when I came to Tonjibe. I struggled all night in prayer and wouldn't let sleep overcome my vigil.

TEN: THE MALEKU MINISTRY

"Lord," I prayed, "if that boy dies, the little bit of faith the poor woman has will be shattered. For that dear woman, please heal that boy."

When I saw the first crack of daylight, I jumped up and made my way to this woman's hut. I was so pleased by what I saw there! The sore on the boy's foot had ruptured and allowed the pus to drain. His skin was wrinkled because the swelling had gone down. Even the redness had subsided. Although the two areas of swelling on the leg were still present, they were doing a God-engineered job of blocking poison from making its way to the heart.

God had done something and I was quite sure he would continue to heal that boy.

It took about two weeks before he was completely healed. The woman, whose name was Joaquina, eventually became a faithful Christian. This boy and his brother later became Christians, too.

Eleven

RETURNING HOME
June 1970–Summer 1971

After two short years in Costa Rica, I decided to go back to Canada. My brother Bill was getting married and had asked if I might return for the wedding. I could speak Spanish quite well by now and felt that I was only beginning to feel capable of speaking freely with the locals about the gospel.

Now that I was returning home, would I ever be back? I didn't know. I knew I had learned a great deal about trusting God on a daily basis. I felt that even if I never went back, everything I had learned in these two years would change my life forever.

I had left Canada with $2,000, a sum that was by now almost totally used up. But I believed that God would provide for my needs. No church group had decided to help me on a regular basis, yet I believed that help would arrive when the fruit of my labour spoke for itself.

I arrived back in Canada to face an uncertain future. Even though I had been trained as an electronic technician, I managed to get a job as an electrician. This was easier to acquire in the short-term.

Who was to say whether God would call me back to Costa Rica, or perhaps elsewhere? The words of 2 Timothy 2:4 were very firmly on my mind: *"No one engaged in warfare entangles himself with the affairs of this life, that he may please him who enlisted him as a soldier"* (NKJV). I believed it was a strong possibility that the Lord had prepared me for something more.

My parents had moved to Trenton, Nova Scotia, which had a flying school at its airport. I decided to attend this school to earn my pilot's license in my spare time. I figured this would come in handy if the Lord called me back to the mission field.

As for my employment situation, I didn't want to apply for any job that might expect me to stay for a long period of time. Even still, after one year of working in Canada I had to wonder whether I would ever go back south.

One night I had a dream about Pedro, one of the believers from down in Costa Rica. The dream was very short and it showed me an image of Pedro looking very downcast or discouraged.

What could this mean?

I certainly couldn't see any way that I could get the time off to go to Costa Rica anytime soon. I was now responsible for two apprentices and reasoned that they would have problems if I were to leave.

After a few more months had passed, work surprisingly became slack. We had several contracts on the books, but they all seemed to be delayed.

Even more surprising, instead of laying off the apprentices my boss, Joe, asked me if I wanted to take a vacation. Wow! And in that moment, the image of Pedro flashed back to my mind.

"If I'm going to take a vacation, I'm going to make good use of it," I said to my boss.

"You go right ahead and do whatever you want to," Joe replied.

"Then I'll go to Costa Rica."

"I have no problem with that."

Joe was a very devoted Christian and seemed to have guessed what was on my mind.

My initial plan was to go to the Air Canada office in Halifax, since I'd had good fortune that way before.

It just so happened that there was going to be a full eclipse of the sun in our area that very day, a very rare occurrence, and many people were flying in from all over to witness it. When I got to the airport in Trenton, which was usually quiet, there was all kinds of commotion. I had hoped to find someone who would be willing to fly me to Halifax, but my hopes were dashed.

Somehow I got into a conversation with a pilot who had just flown in from Delaware. He definitely wasn't flying to Halifax, though, because the best place to view the eclipse was right at the Trenton airport.

Instead, this pilot offered to take me back to Delaware with his family. He would be leaving the next morning. Wow! And I would even get to stay and watch the eclipse. Does God ever put frosting on the cake? He sure does!

When I arrived in Delaware the next day, I booked a flight to carry on down to Costa Rica. It was really a wonderful experience.

When I got to Costa Rica, not only did I see a real need with Pedro, but everywhere I went I felt a sense of urgency. But how could I consider staying? I had the responsibility of two apprentices.

"Lord," I prayed, "if you want me to stay, help me to know for sure."

I sent a letter to Joe, explaining the situation. I reasoned that this letter might take too long, so then I sent a telegram. I reasoned further, though, that I needed to hear from him even sooner. However, using the phone would be expensive.

Having no choice, I placed the call.

After explaining what had happened, Joe told me, "You do whatever you think God wants you to do. Don't worry about a thing here. Everything is under my control."

Well, that was an answer to prayer! I now believed that I should stay in Costa Rica.

This stay, though, would turn out to be much different than the first, because by now the Teigrobs had moved back to Canada.

Around this time, I received a letter from the People's Church in New Glasgow, Nova Scotia, which was close to my former home in

Trenton. They informed me that they were going to trust God for an offering of $50 per month. As it turned out, I received $100 per month from them for two years, praise the Lord.

I decided that my best plan was to remain permanently in the lowlands. I set up an itinerary to visit each palenque on a particular day of the week to conduct a service, so the people there would know when to expect me. The rest of the time, I would be flexible to be wherever I was called upon to be.

When I found out that someone was selling a chainsaw for a low price, I bought it. I expected that there must be something wrong with it, and indeed it turned out to have a gas leak. Also, the leak was coming from down inside the machine. Very few people there had any knowledge of mechanics and wouldn't venture to tear it apart to try fixing it. And it would be quite an ordeal to take it all the way out to the city.

I took a chance on it being fixable. After I pulled it apart, I noticed a rubber gasket that had been poorly installed. I put it back together and afterward that chainsaw became the envy of everyone in the area.

There were no sawmills nearby, so people had to saw logs into lumber with chainsaws. After watching how they did this, I also got the hang of it—although I could do so with far less fuel since my chainsaw was smaller than everyone else's.

Lumber was a real need, since houses had to be built. The frame of a house could be made much straighter with two-by-fours rather than round natural poles from trees. The boarded walls fit more tightly and the boarded floors were huge improvements over mud floors.

Yes, having this chainsaw was a major asset. I also used it to cut logs into fence posts, as some of the Maleku were trying to get started in raising cattle.

I also needed a better means of transportation. Walking was laboursome in the rainy season—and when I went out with my chainsaw, I often carried four gallons of gas and tools.

I heard about a black horse that was being auctioned, so I bid on it and got it for a very low price. It had one serious fault, however; someone had abused it and it had a great sore in the middle of its back. I treated the sore and then put it out to pasture at Pedro's farm.

The horse took six months to heal, although there was no hair where the sore had been and the skin was very fragile. After saddling it up, even exercising the best of care, I realized I would need to leave it in the pasture for another week to restore its back.

One day Pedro offered me a deal. He would trade my *fuste* (a cowboy's working saddle) for his *montura* (a horse rider's saddle). The *fuste* was much cheaper and had no horn in the front. The *montura* was built much higher in the front, allowing it to clear the horse's back and shoulders.

Pedro needed the *fuste* to handle his cattle. And as he pointed out to me, his *montura* wouldn't continue to chafe where the *fuste* had.

That trade made every difference in the world. Now I could even run with the horse.

And what a horse it was! I told people it had power steering. When you held the rein to one side so the rope touched the side of its neck, it turned that way. When I gave a slight pull back, it backed up. A little more of a tug and it would stand up on its hindlegs.

In its younger days, this horse must have had excellent training. It was difficult to catch in the pasture, but if I threw a rope just over its neck it would stop short. I usually got it to come to me with bananas or salt. However, that trick didn't seem to work with the cowboys.

Twelve

PLANE CRASH
1970

Henry was a very brave man, in my opinion, but I believe he was brave because he trusted God. He had a winsome personality, too, which was a great asset in the ministry. He was also a bit of a horse trader in that he could buy something and sell it at a profit, a trait that I never learned from him. He could have been a millionaire, I believe, if he had chosen to do so, but instead he gave his energies to spread the gospel and forged a trail for the gospel among the Maleku.

Above all, he was an example to me and I will be forever indebted to him.

While I was in Canada working and training to be a pilot, we got some frightening news that Henry, Anne, and their son James had survived a very serious plane crash. At the time, we heard very few details of the accident except that they had survived with minor injuries.

"Praise the Lord," I said upon hearing the news.

Someone nearby retorted, "If it hadn't been for Henry's skill, they could have all been killed."

I said nothing more but thought it wrong not to give credit to God.

Later I heard the details of what had happened. Henry had gotten clearance to take off in San José with the understanding that the pass over the mountain range was clear. He took off with his Cessna-150, a very light plane when it came to flying in mountainous areas, and flew towards the pass.

He was with Anne and little James, who was sitting on her lap. Anne had a seatbelt but James's only physical protection were the two arms wrapped around him.

As they neared the pass, a bank of clouds crowded in very quickly. Henry thought of returning to San José, but upon turning around he could see that the clouds were also closing in behind him. At that point, he believed that he had better try to proceed towards the pass, lowering his altitude so as to stay below the cloud cover.

He approached the pass, flying dangerously close to the rugged terrain below. Even at full throttle, the plane was losing altitude due to a strong downdraft. That was when Henry realized that he wasn't going to make it through. His only option was to turn around and try his luck in the opposite direction.

However, he didn't have enough room to manoeuvre around, and if he tried making a steep turn he knew he could stall.

And that's exactly what happened. The plane stalled as Henry attempted to do a 180-degree turn.

After a plane stalls, the pilot is no longer in control. The plane dove towards the ground, flipped upside-down, and came to a stop at the bottom of a wedge-shaped ravine.

Henry and Anne were hanging upside-down by their seatbelts. While Anne struggled to hang on to James, Henry managed to loosen his seatbelt. He grabbed James and helped Anne get out of her seatbelt as well. They then scrambled out of one of the doors and along the wing. The big concern was the potential for a fire to break out, so they made their way up the ravine, away from the plane, and into the jungle.

They hadn't gone far before they came to a clearing where they stopped to thank the Lord for sparing their lives. After looking around the field, they noticed a farmhouse and made their way towards it. Henry had some soreness in his chest and Anne had a sore arm, but none of these symptoms turned out to be serious. James, who been wrapped in the loving arms of his mother, fared the best of the three.

The plane had been totally destroyed, but otherwise everyone was fine. The Teigrobs returned to Canada shortly after.

Thirteen

CHAINSAW WORK AND HORSE TRAVEL
1971–1973

One day I went over to a village called Patasti to assist in a service. The man who had invited me spoke of a problem they had in the village. Heavy rains had taken out a nearby bridge and the children had to walk a long way around to get to school every day. The people had been waiting a long time for someone to come and build a new bridge, but no one had yet offered to do it.

The man explained that he had trees cut down that just needed to be cut into planks to build the bridge. I agreed to do that for him.

When I showed up with my little chainsaw, however, he was sceptical. He didn't say a word and proceeded to show me a tree that had been cut down years earlier but hadn't rotted because of the type of wood. He wanted this tree cut into three beams to support the bridge.

This wasn't difficult with my twenty-three-inch blade because the trunk wasn't terribly big.

For the planks, this man showed me a few huge tree logs that someone had already cut into twelve-foot lengths, each one being three and a half feet across. He was wondering how I was going to accomplish this.

I climbed up onto one of the logs and made two small notches at the top of each end. I ran a cord the length of the log using twigs to anchor the ends in the notches. Then, holding the saw so the blade was perpendicular to the ground, I proceeded to make a four-inch cut located one inch from the cord. The cord served to show a straight line. After that, I removed the cord and proceeded to deepen the cut about four inches at a time.

Eventually I had the saw vertical with the full length of the blade in the log. Since this only reached to the centre of the log, with the man's help we rolled the log over until the cut was at the bottom, perpendicular with the ground. Then I climbed up on the log again and did the same. When I reached the centre, both halves rolled apart. That moment was a bit precarious!

I continued to cut the halves into planks. Then the man apologized to me, although he had nothing to apologize for. He admitted that when he'd seen my small saw, he hadn't thought I would be able to do it. I told him that where there is a need, God provides a way.

Travelling by horse had its advantages, but there were also disadvantages. You always had to have a place to pasture the horse when you stayed someplace overnight. Another thing was that you may think you can be high and dry sitting on horseback, but sometimes you're in for surprises. If the horse happens to put a front foot into another horse's print hole, water escaping from that hole can shoot straight up and get you dirtier than if you had walked.

If it should rain, I had the option of wearing a *capa*, a specially made raincoat for horse riding. This coat was made long on the sides and short on the front and back. That didn't work well for me if I had any wooden culverts to cross. My horse had a fear of wooden bridges or culverts. I always had to dismount and walk slightly ahead of the horse, letting him take the time to smell the bridge, then after one or two steps walk straight across. However, if it is pouring rain, the *capa* was too long on the sides to keep it out of the mud, so I'd have to remove it while attempting to get the horse across. By that time, I could be soaking wet.

THIRTEEN: CHAINSAW WORK AND HORSE TRAVEL

Sometimes I had to cross huge swamp holes. Some horses weren't made for swamps, especially when they would sink to their bellies in mud. A good horse would stop and move one foot at a time until it crossed. A poor horse might start jumping, knock the rider off, and may even end up on its side in the mud hole. Fortunately, my horse was good for mud holes.

I travelled quite a bit on horseback, in all kinds of weather, but one particular trip stands out as perhaps the most enjoyable. After a service one night, I headed out on a journey to a village called El Venado (The Deer) with a man I had quite recently met. As we chatted, he shared his testimony. He had belonged to a religious group that required its followers to do a lot visiting and write up reports of all the visits. When he had gotten behind in his reports, the group had threatened to remove him. That hadn't rung true to him, to lose out on heaven on account of paperwork, so he'd decided to check out the Latin American mission which had a church in his village. Eventually, he and his wife had accepted Jesus Christ as their Lord and Saviour. He was so thankful that he had come to see the light of Christ.

As we meandered along in the moonlight that night, he started singing Christian songs he knew from memory. It was such a peaceful and satisfying experience. His excellent voice reminded me of something I might only see in the movies.

On another occasion, Pedro asked if he could borrow my horse to run an errand since his horses were already hard-worked and needed time to rest and feed. I didn't have any problem with that as long as he could be back before three o'clock in the afternoon, because I had an important errand to take care of in Guatuso. He intended to be back long before that, so off he went with my horse.

The day wore on and three o'clock arrived—but no horse. Four o'clock arrived and still no horse.

Finally, at five o'clock Pedro arrived with the horse.

I wasn't happy, but instead of saying something I waited for him to speak first. He started off by apologizing for having come so late. I had assumed he hadn't realized how important my appointment was. I wondered whether he really had tried to get back sooner.

I don't remember what his excuse was, but I should have forgiven him since he was a brother in Christ and had apologized.

"It's okay," I told him. But deep down, it wasn't okay.

I got on the horse and headed for Guatuso. As soon as I was out of sight, I began to beat the horse so that it ran at full gallop. All the time, my conscience was telling me that I shouldn't take out my frustration on the horse. None of this was the horse's fault.

I came to a place where the path split in two. The horse took the path I hadn't intended to take, but I knew that the two paths rejoined a bit later on. If I pulled the horse up short in order to get on the other path, I would lose more time than it would take to continue on the longer route.

Seconds later the horse sprinted under the limbs of a tree that had a huge hornet's nest. They started stinging me straightaway, so I rolled off the horse's back and landed in the tall grass, where I stayed until the hornets dissipated.

Surprisingly, the horse only ran on its own a short distance before stopping as if to wait for me.

"Okay, Lord," I said as I picked up my sombrero. "I hear you and I'm sorry."

I walked over to the horse, got on its back, and walked all the way to Guatuso. What I couldn't get done that day would have to wait for another day.

Sometimes the Lord didn't talk *through* me to others but rather *to* me.

THIRTEEN: CHAINSAW WORK AND HORSE TRAVEL

My little black horse

Fourteen

GAINING TRUST AND EVEN DEPENDENCE

One rainy evening, as we were finishing a service, the congregation and I heard a strange noise. Many of our neighbours heard it as well and we all went out to investigate. We found a pig in distress and assumed that a cow had kicked it when it had gotten too close.

The neighbours decided to shoot it and take it out of its misery.

"It will have to be dressed as well," I said after the deed was done. "We can't wait until morning to dress it."

So who was going to dress it? I expected one of them to offer, but no one did. Instead they just looked to me. I didn't have much experience, especially at night with nothing but a candle for light and in spitting rain.

When you dress any animal, you do the opposite of what it sounds like; you remove the hide or hair, as in the case of a pig, and then open it up to remove the insides. It's important to do this early on or the meat will spoil.

They lifted the animal onto a cow's salt bench which had some curve to it so it wouldn't roll off too easily. We decided to skip shaving the hair for now and instead do that in the daylight.

It would have been easier if we could have strung it up somewhere, but we made do and finished dressing the animal at about one o'clock in the morning.[2] We finished it up the next day, but it definitely wasn't as easy to shave a dressed animal, as the empty carcass tended to cave inwards.

One day, a boy came to me with a two-inch splinter in his leg. It had almost come through the other side. What could I do? I wasn't a doctor.

I had cured my horse when its front shoulder had been badly swollen and the wound filled with maggots. I had just cleaned the wound and stuffed the hole full of cow salve. The next day, the dead maggots had all fallen out. After cleaning it again, I had treated it the same way as before. The swelling went down and the shoulder healed in no time.

This was different, of course, being a human.

As a first step, I asked for God's help to deal with this boy's problem. I then managed to get the large splinter out, but the pus was dark green. I wondered how long the splinter had been in there. I filled the hole with cow salve,[3] like my horse, and bandaged it up.

"I want to see you tomorrow," I told him firmly afterward.

He showed up the next day and I removed as much debris as I could, but already the pus was a better colour, without any solid green substance inside. I filled it with cow salve again and rebandaged it.

People somehow trusted me even more than I trusted myself. When they saw me coming, they often ran out and asked me to pray for them. Sometimes it would just be for a fever or a cold; other times it would be more serious. I always asked for them to get me some cooking oil or something to represent the Holy Spirit, stressing that only God can heal.

Later, upon coming back past their place, I often didn't want to see them. Due to my lack in faith, I expected them to still be ill. Instead they would come running out to tell me that they were all better.

---

2 During this process, I noticed an embolism in the pig's lungs that backed up our suspicion that it had been kicked by the cow.

3 Cow salve is similar to the salves that are sold for human use, but a little stronger.

FOURTEEN: GAINING TRUST AND EVEN DEPENDENCE

On another occasion, a man lay ill on a slab on the floor of his hut. He had sent word for me to come and give him an injection of penicillin. Evidently he had received injections before but needed someone to administer another one now. I had never given injections before and didn't know anything about it, but he insisted and bared his back side.

Well, either his skin was as tough as cowhide or the needle was dull. I think both were true. I pushed and pushed until finally the needle penetrated the skin. He never complained, even though it must have hurt.

I checked the needle outdoors in good light and could see that the point was shiny, indicating that the needle had probably been used many times before. I hoped it had been properly sterilized.

Another night, I visited a home where the children were outside playing hide-and-seek while us adults talked inside. Suddenly we heard a scream and crying. Everyone went out with to see what had happened.

Someone had thought to bring a flashlight and shone it on a boy who stood next to a post. The prong of a fence staple was sticking out of the wood on one side, and I guessed that the boy had grabbed the post to support a quick change of direction only for the staple to pierce him between the thumb and forefinger. The staple went right through and out the other side. Because the fence post was made of very hard wood, the staple wouldn't come out easily.

I approached, explaining that I wanted to have a look at it, and very gently placed my right hand under his. Then, as quick as a flash, I brought his hand around and up off the staple. He started to holler but stopped abruptly as he realized he was free of the staple.

I thanked the Lord, because I knew that I wouldn't have had a second chance at this.

One day Pedro and I were walking through the jungle. As I led, I saw what looked like a round stick about two to three inches thick laying across the narrow path. I stepped on it, and as I lowered my weight onto it my brain started to realize that this wasn't a stick.

I jumped back suddenly, bumping into Pedro. Instead of being frightened like I was, he burst out laughing. From his vantage point he could see the rest of this huge black snake, which scrambled to make its way out of there. It took me a few seconds before I could join him in the laughing spree.

He and I spent many hours at night exchanging stories. I would tell a story from my industrialized background and he would tell one from his jungle background. Our backgrounds were so different, yet our stories had a lot in common. How could that be? I could reach only one conclusion: we had both been designed by the same God. This fortified my belief that the Bible is the true account of our beginning. We both came from Adam.

One night as I chatted with him during the night, the house began to creak.

"What's that?" I asked him.

"Oh, it's just the pig scratching himself on one of the house posts."

A bit later, we heard the same creaking sound, only louder this time. I asked the same question.

"Oh, it's likely the horse scratching himself on the house."

Unsatisfied with this answer, I jumped up and walked out to the corridor. I shouted to him that the horse was way over by the edge of the lot.

"Okay then," he said. "It must be an earthquake."

He didn't seem to get very excited about it, since the nearby Arenal volcano had been making more and more noises lately. Nothing serious had happened with that volcano since its last major eruption in 1986, shortly before I had come to Costa Rica.

People started coming to me with their broken chainsaws, or whatever machine they had, to help with repairs. One man came to me on a number of occasions with items that, had he undertaken even a simple investigation, he could have fixed himself and saved himself a lot of trouble. Sometimes, when his chainsaw gave him trouble, he finished the day swinging the axe and then brought it to me to take a look.

When you know very little about something, you assume you can't fix it before you even start. Often you won't attempt to look for the problem.

FOURTEEN: GAINING TRUST AND EVEN DEPENDENCE

With this guy, I had standing joke: "If only you had used your head, you wouldn't have had to use your muscle."

I used that on him a few times, but one time it backfired on me. It turned out, in this case, that I was the one who had failed to do a simple thing that could have avoided a lot of extra trouble. The laugh was on me.

One day I had to go out to the city. Pedro and his cousin Leonel wanted to borrow my chainsaw while I was away. Unfortunately, I don't think they got much done with it before the saw gave them some problems. They decided to get the bag of tools which I used to repair saws and struggled for quite a while without success.

"We're lacking one thing," Leonel piped up after a bit.

"What's that?" asked Pedro.

"La cabeza de Dónal," he replied. (Donald's head).

They had a hearty laugh and then brought the saw back to the house.

Another thing the people looked up to me for was shooting iguanas. I wasn't an archer by any means, but on one occasion I agreed to go on a hunting and fishing trip with a couple of the Maleku named Charía and Nicanor. We fished as we travelled down the Rio Frio, a much larger river than El Sol which emptied into it.

At one point, Charía decided that he would go hunting while Nicanor and I carried on fishing from where the boat, which was tied up.

From time to time we had heard shots ringing out. This went on for quite a while and finally I said to Nicanor, "He must have a lot of meat by now."

"Let's go and see," Nicanor replied.

We didn't have any trouble finding him, because all we had to do was keep walking in the direction of the shots.

When we got there, Charía came right over to me with the .22 rifle and handed it to me.

"Please shoot the iguana," he said to me.

I looked up into the tree and couldn't see anything. I then gave the gun to Nicanor, who fired. Nothing came down.

Charía fired again—and still nothing happened.

"It's no use," I said when they tried to give the rifle back to me. "I can't see it."

"Stand right behind me," Nicanor said.

When I did, he instructed me to let my eyes follow up the barrel of the gun as he pointed at the animal.

Suddenly, I saw a tiny black silhouette that appeared to be the size of a small lizard.

"Oh, that's too small," I remarked. "You don't want to shoot an animal that small."

"No," they said in unison. "That is *big*." They demonstrated with outstretched arms.

Could it be, I thought, *that this animal is so high up in tree that it only appears small?*

I decided to give it a try. I fired and the little silhouette ran for a distance atop the tree and stopped again. Nicanor and Charía each took another shot at it, but it never moved.

This is crazy. Almost a box of shells is gone and still not one piece of meat.

I found a two-pronged, Y-shaped stick and stuck it in the ground. Then I lowered one knee and put the barrel of the gun in the crook of the Y. I took my time, eased back on the trigger… and *bang*. Down it came.

When the iguana hit the ground, I couldn't believe my eyes. *Whoomph!* It wasn't small and it wasn't black. It was orange with black stripes and was at least six feet long.

Well, you can imagine who people looked for to shoot their iguanas after that! I still wasn't any good at spotting them, though. They could spot them as quick as a wink. It's just that they had a terrible time actually shooting them. I never could understand that.

One time, a group of six of us went hunting iguanas on horseback. Eventually we got to a certain spot in the jungle where we stopped and tied up our horses. After walking through the underbrush a bit, they decided to climb a big tree to shoot down iguanas.

"How do you know there are any iguanas up there?" I asked.

They proceeded to show me what looked like milk stains on the leaves nearest the ground. They said this was an indication that there were a lot of iguanas up in that tree.

Together we moved to a spot with a clearer view of the top branches. As I peered upwards, I noticed a little black silhouette right at the top of this tall tree.

They yanked down on various vines until they found one they were satisfied with. One guy used it shimmy up to the lowest branches, approximately fifty feet up. Then another man shimmied up. The others sought out smaller vines by which they could haul up the two men's guns.

Soon they were out of sight in the plumage of leaves.

Myself and one other were responsible to get to the place where they fell. A shot would sound, then we'd hear the sound of an iguana coming down through the trees and run towards it—usually not the one shot at, but another that was startled by the noise of the gunshot.

Every iguana that hit the ground still alive instantly scurried off towards the river, but we had two people assigned to stand at the river's edge and try to catch them. We'd hear one splash followed by two more splashes as the men gave chase. Not one iguana that made a run for the river got away.

After some time, the tree climbers were tired and came down—even though there were still more iguanas up there. They'd had enough.

Once they had shimmied back down the vine, we counted the iguanas and there was one short of three apiece for each of us, so I agreed to only take two.

While they got busy tying the iguanas onto their horses, I took a stroll over to see if I could find the original little black silhouette at the top of the tall tree. Sure enough, it was exactly where we'd left it.

No one was paying attention to me, so I found another Y-shaped stick, aimed up with the rifle, and eased back on the trigger. Down it came.

Everyone seemed to holler at once: "Hermano Dónal shot another one!"

It fell to the ground dead—and now I had three as well.

Fifteen

FRUSTRATION, DISCOURAGEMENT, ILLNESS, AND QUESTIONS

He who continually goes forth weeping, bearing seed for sowing, shall doubtless come again with rejoicing, bringing his sheaves with him. (Psalm 126:6, NKJV)

During my time in Costa Rica, a few young people from the palenques appeared to respond to the gospel, and some even followed through in baptism. However, the world and the pressure put on them to return to drinking was, for the most part, overpowering. The older folks wanted to get the young back into their old ways. Why? It didn't make any sense. When they had followed Christ, everything about their lives had changed: their health, their hygiene, their homes, and their work.

On a return visit to Tonjibe, I went to see a man named Francisco, as he had made a decision to follow Christ. He seemed to be ready for baptism and I thought his example would be a great encouragement for his brother, Ramiro.

In speaking with Francisco, I went through every passage of the Bible several times that dealt with baptism—and no, it turned out that he wasn't ready to be baptized. Why? Because he had seen so many of his fellow Maleku slip back into the world of sin and strong drink. He wasn't going to do that and make a fool of himself, disgrace the gospel, and bring the name of the Lord under reproach. He was going to be sure of the truth of the gospel before he was to be identified with it.

On a short visit from Canada, Henry also tried to get him to go ahead with baptism but to no avail. He just wasn't ready.

I was quite happy with what was happening in El Sol and Tonjibe. God was working in these palenques. But in spite of all the progress Henry had made earlier with the gospel in Margarita, there was a great amount of backsliding there. Frustration and discouragement was setting in.

I also suffered plenty of illness during this period. It seemed as though I would just be getting over one thing when another would hit me. I struggled with many different parasites, as parasitic infections were as common as the common cold. Diarrhea, too, was a constant battle. And I always lived under the threat of tuberculosis or malaria.

A Hispanic believer must have seen the frustration on my face.

"Brother Don, you are wasting your time with these native people," he said to me. "You will never have a church among these people. They are like a piece of soft wire. You come along and they bend one way. A catholic priest comes along and they bend another way. You should leave these people and come and work among us Hispanics. Then you will have a church."

Well, that was both encouraging and troublesome at the same time.

Now if you can appreciate what I've just written, you can understand how tempted I was to agree with him.

He may have seemed right, but first of all we know *"that God is no respecter of persons"* (Acts 10:34). Therefore if one of these native people sincerely trusted and accepted Jesus Christ as their Lord and Saviour, he would come and make his dwelling with that person and continue with him. Philippians 1:6 also said, *"being confident of this very thing, that He who has begun a good work in you will complete it until the day of Jesus Christ"* (NKJV).

"God led me to the Maleku through brother Henry, and I cannot leave them until God gives leave to do so," I told this man.

FIFTEEN: FRUSTRATION, DISCOURAGEMENT, ILLNESS AND QUESTIONS

This wasn't the only pressure put on me to leave the Maleku. A pastor from a church in Canada which had been supporting me for over a year came to visit in Costa Rica. Everywhere we went, we experienced blessings.

"One thing I am sure of," he said to me. "The Lord has called you to the mission field."

Yet when he returned to Canada and talked it over with the church leadership, they recommended for me to go elsewhere to start a church. Knowing that they would continue to support me if I was willing to follow their recommendations, I felt a great deal of pressure to leave the Maleku.

What was holding me there? I had no personal reason to want to stay.

I struggled earnestly in prayer. "Lord, if you want me to go elsewhere, show me. I am willing to go where you want me to go. Lord, you know what others are saying I should do, and you know how illness has been hindering the ministry here. If you want me to stay, show me that you want me to stay. And show me that you can continue to use me to speak to these people. Lord, you know how many have turned back from following you. Thank you, Lord."

The first sign I got was a change in my health. After this, nine months went by without feeling illness of any sort—and even when I did get sick, it was only a slight cold. That was a pretty strong leading. I believe that God was working through my ministry all along, even though I hadn't been able to see it at first.

Francisco followed through with baptism and remained faithful. I don't know of any occasion when he turned back. His brother, and eventually most of the family, came to trust the Lord Jesus as their Saviour—even his mother and father, which was very unusual for the older folks in any of the villages. Most of the people there who had turned away from Christ eventually fell under conviction and emerged victorious over the temptations of the world, resurrendering their lives to God. They had a great desire to tell me that they were back serving the Lord.

Others didn't resurrender until long after I had left the country. Still, when I came back for visits they praised the Lord for the opportunity to tell me that they had claimed victory over the slavery of sin.

Sixteen

A SKEPTICAL FARMER
1972

One year after returning to Costa Rica, I had gotten quite well acclimatized to living full-time at close to sea level. I had a lot on the go and people sought me out very often.

There was a farmer in the area who was a very strong Roman Catholic and he believed the evangelicals were wrong. But he had a problem.

He and another man had gone out to San José and bought themselves new fumigators, machines that are mounted on a person's back and used to churn up a mixture of insecticide into a fog-like vapour that can be sprayed onto crops. They most likely took the six-hour journey by horseback to Tilarán, followed by a five-hour bus ride to the city. After making their purchases, they would have had to come back the same way.

When they got back to their farms, neither of their fumigators would start—and they weren't prepared to go all the way back to return these machines. This farmer didn't like to have anything to do with evangelicals, but word had gotten around that I fixed chainsaws and the like, so he traced me down.

He didn't start talking about the true reason for his visit, but rather, almost immediately, criticized some of the "foolish" things evangelicals believe. When I tried to defend one issue, he quickly switched to another. I couldn't say much on any issue before he'd cut me off with something else.

I realized early on that I would have to let him wind down before he'd give me a chance to speak.

Before he did, however, he switched to the reason for his coming. He told me about his machine and asked if I could come and take a look at it. I told him that I couldn't look at it for two weeks because I had company coming from Canada. He was very much disappointed that I couldn't look at it sooner.

Henry soon arrived and we spent the next two weeks travelling together. Not only had I been keeping regular services in the palenques, but I was also assisting in other Hispanic villages where I was asked either to speak or to fix something.

We went to Patasti for a service, but afterward we needed to return by a different route. The trail led us over some sizable hills. I realized that Henry wasn't as acclimatized as I was, having come straight from Canada, so I walked slowly even though he usually walked at a pretty good pace. Even then, he asked me to slow down more.

A bit later, he called again for me to slow down.

Then, after a while longer, he shouted, "Stop!" By this time, though, I was already going so slow that I was almost stopped anyway.

The shoe is on the other foot now, I thought to myself.

Anyway, God really blessed everyone while he was there and he was quite encouraged to see how the work was coming along.

A short time after Henry had returned to Canada, the other man who had purchased a fumigator came over to ask me to look at his machine. I went over to his place one morning and examined his fumigator. After pulling the cord a few times, I checked the spark plug and found it wet. I then checked the throttle needle and it was extended as far as it could go, meaning that the amount of gas getting to the motor was set at minimum.

I then explained to him that the motor was flooding at its minimum setting and the only way to reduce it further would be to make another notch in the needle to close off more of the gas intake. However, I didn't want to make changes to his brand-new machine.

"Go ahead and do it, if you think that will help," he said.

After making that change, the motor started and ran well—except that when I released the trigger to let it idle, it would quickly stop. When I examined the spark plug again, it was again wet. I examined the carburetor closely and could make no adjustment to allow extra air in while the motor was idling.

"Most of the motors I've worked on have a slash cutaway on the throttle cylinder that regulates the amount of air the motor receives in the idle position," I said. "When you pull the trigger, the cylinder and needle move up together. On idle, the motor needs easier access to more air to avoid flooding."

I didn't want to mess with his new machine, but the only suggestion I could make was to cut a slash piece off the bottom of the air intake cylinder.

"You go ahead and do whatever you think," he said.

I admired his confidence in me. After making the change, the machine worked like a charm.

When the first man heard about this fix, he tried to do the same thing to his own fumigator. But it was to no avail.

Eventually, he once again asked me to look at his machine. I went over first thing on a Monday morning. The motor had no recognizable symptoms, so I proceeded by testing it in a systematic way. I started to check for the continuity of contact through the points.

"Oh, there is nothing wrong with the points, because I put new points in it," he said.

Well, there shouldn't have been anything wrong with the points that had come with the machine, but this made me wonder what else he may have altered.

"I have a procedure I follow," I told him. "I check everything in a certain order."

He allowed me to proceed.

Shortly into my work, I remarked, "Your new points are touching, but they aren't making contact."

After removing them, I showed him the points; they were rusted. And that wasn't the only problem. I worked on his machine all day and fixed five faults, all of them the result of his own attempts to fix the machine.

Now the motor would start, but it would rev up and down by itself and then quit. The truth is that I was stumped, but I didn't tell him that.

At one point, he came over from the house and said that his wife had prepared supper for me. They also had a bed for me to stay night, so I could get back to work on the fumigator the next day. I had nothing pressing, so I agreed.

After supper, he said something that very much surprised me: would I read from the Bible? Well, I was more than glad to! I reached for my Bible in my satchel.

"No," he said. "My Bible."

I was okay with that and reached out my hand for his Bible.

"I will choose the passage," he said.

He opened the Bible to the book of Isaiah. Right there was the gospel, so I explained it to him from the passage he had selected.

I went to bed on a canvas scissor bed; it wasn't soft, but at least it was a whole lot softer than hardwood boards. I struggled in prayer for the answer as to why the motor had acted the way it had, but I also prayed for this man and his family, that somehow they might see the truth of the gospel.

Early in the morning, as the sky was brightening with light, God put an idea in my head. I ran out to the barn and took apart the machine's carburetor. I removed the throttle needle this man had modified and examined it closely. That's when I noticed that the groove hadn't been made smoothly. I cleared it out with a hacksaw blade and then put the carburetor back together.

The motor worked perfectly.

What idea had come to my mind? A gasoline motor vibrates a certain amount, and this vibration causes the throttle needle to turn around and around. The gas coming up the needle actually spirals up the needle because the needle turns. It had occurred to me that if the needle cannot turn freely, it would throw off the gas intake, producing erratic results.

The man came out of the house with a smile on his face.

"Last night I didn't know what was wrong with your machine," I told him. "So I asked God to help me to figure out what was wrong. This morning, God enabled me to find the fault with your machine."

He was obviously pleased and I went on my way.

I never saw this man again, but others told me what he had been saying about his encounter with me: "If anyone was going to convert me, it would be that gringo." I didn't mind the rude title. I was just pleased that God had touched him somewhat.

Seventeen

EARTHQUAKE
April 1973

For the first time, I chose to return to Guatuso overland by Tilarán instead of travelling by air from Ciudad Quesada. It was the dry season and the people had brought in a dozer to open the road, allowing trucks to transport supplies and take crops out.

There was usually a month or two of dependable dry weather between March and May, and the locals would just scrape the trails enough to enable vehicles to travel. Rivers had to be forded, but people could usually find a shallow place to cross.

It took me about five hours by bus to get to Tilarán. It was obvious that people were trying to take advantage of the temporary roads because there was a lot of commotion on the streets and every hotel I could find was already full. I wasn't too concerned, though, because I believed that God would provide for me somehow.

When I saw a café across the street, I decided to go there to think about my situation and pray.

I walked in and, to my surprise, saw Luis Cruz from Tonjibe sitting at a table. I joined him for a cup of coffee.

"Where are you staying?" Luis asked.

"I don't know yet."

"Do you think you'll find a place?"

"I don't know. I've checked a few places, but they were full."

"After we have our coffee, I'll find a place for you," Luis said assuredly.

I thought maybe he knew of some hotels which I hadn't seen in the area.

After we had finished our coffee, he led the way to a couple of hotels I had tried already. When we confirmed that they were full, I followed him to yet another hotel. But instead of going to the desk, he walked straight up the stairs.

"Where are you going?" I asked, unable to figure out what he was up to.

"Never mind. Just follow me." He then opened a room door and said, "There is your bed."

"No! Where are you going to sleep?"

"On the floor."

"No, this is your room…"

"Listen," Luis said with a smile on his face. "Don't argue with me. I'm more accustomed to sleeping on the floor than you are."

What more could I say? The room was small with a very narrow cot. Back in Tonjibe, I had spent some time helping Luis read the Bible and I always felt sorry for him because his reading was so laboursome. By the time he finished a sentence, I expected that he would have forgotten the first part of the sentence. On the contrary, though, he seemed to retain more of what he'd read than those who could read much faster.

Anyway, we lay down to rest but carried on talking. He told me about a nerve problem he had. Whenever something sudden happened, he got a spasm that took some time to go away. I shared a number of scriptures with him and talked until we both dropped off to sleep at about one o'clock in the morning.

At about four o'clock, the little cot started to shake violently. I grabbed both sides of the cot to make sure I didn't fall off. I knew right away that this was an earthquake and I thought about whether the building would remain standing. Realizing that it was built from lumber rather than concrete blocks definitely provided some consolation.

The quake lasted about twenty seconds, after which I suddenly thought of Luis, who had not moved or made a sound. Was he still sleeping or had something serious happened to him?

I reached down to his chest to shake him.

"It's okay," he assured me. "I'm all right."

"But you told me last night that you have a nerve problem."

"Yes, but after the conversation we had last night, for some reason it didn't happen this time."

Praise the Lord!

While we were talking, we heard all kinds of commotion going on out in the hallway. There were shouts, people crying, and sounds of people on the move.

Suddenly, another quake hit. This one once again lasted for about twenty seconds. We just hung on to whatever was close by.

Afterward all the noises subsided. Everyone had left the hotel by this time, so we decided that we should do the same. We got out onto the fire escape landing and looked down at all the people standing in a semicircle in total silence.

Then a third quake hit. We hung onto the steel rail and I watched the houses as they appeared to wobble from side to side. It reminded me of a time years ago when I'd stood at the junction of two railway cars as the train moved down the track. One car would wobble one direction while the one behind it wobbled the other direction.

"Let's go down and talk to the people to help them overcome the shock," I said.

Luis agreed, so we made our way down the stairs and began talking with the people. Soon we noticed a mood change. Fire trucks and police cars appeared on the streets, too, with there sirens going. Soon dump trucks went by, apparently to assist in refilling cracks that had shown up in the roads.

Once the sun had come up, we ventured down the streets to see some of the damage. Most of the cement block buildings were either severally damaged or destroyed. Even some of the wooden houses hadn't held up. The end of one building had tipped out onto the street so we could see into it as though it was a huge dollhouse.

The stained-glass windows in the Catholic church, which had just undergone major renovations, was spread out on the ground. Its concrete walls were covered in cracks.

Out in the country, a landslide had buried two houses and taken the lives of eleven people.

There wasn't much we could do, as we had no place to stay or anywhere to buy food. One proprietor offered us to help ourselves to whatever we wanted to eat. Everything that had been on his shelves was now piled two feet high on the floor.

Soon a car approached and stopped nearby. A woman got out with her daughter and it was obvious that they were quite frightened. She had fled her house only to fall into a crevice up to her waist. She'd scrambled out of the crevice, losing her shoes in the process, and now she was barefoot.

"Why didn't you go back and try to fetch the shoes?" I asked, perhaps trying to lighten the mood a little bit.

"Oh no, no, no, no!" she exclaimed. "I wouldn't go back there. The ground might open up and swallow me alive."

This made us laugh afterwards, but it wasn't really funny at all.

We needed to get back home, but most truckers were nervous of driving along the dozed roads in case there were more quakes. Besides, the rainy season would return soon.

We linked up with a few more people who were hoping for a ride in that direction and finally found a driver brave enough to take us about two-thirds of the way. We all chipped in to pay the driver and away we went.

When we arrived and had offloaded, the driver wasted no time in heading back towards the safer year-round roads.

Our next task was to wade across a fair-sized river, then proceed on foot. By the end of the day, we had made it back to Margarita. Everyone went their separate ways from there. Luis continued up to Tonjibe while I headed in the opposite direction to El Sol.

God had watched over us and I treasured the opportunity I'd had with Luis.

Years later, my wife Grace and I went down for a visit and I arranged to meet up with Luis, whom I hadn't seen on my last two trips to Cosa Rica. He had suffered great physical disability and had many setbacks in trying to set up a cattle ranch.

Luis's house was located quite a ways up from Tonjibe. Because Grace would have had difficulty walking there, Luis's daughter entertained us in her house. She was too young to remember me from when I'd lived there.

Grace had a very good conversation with this daughter, who not only came to trust the Lord but became very involved in the work of the Lord. She was so excited when she found out that I had brought the gospel to her village many years earlier. About three-quarters of the villagers now confessed Jesus as their Lord and Saviour.

I must say, though, that many others have planted and watered in that area since. Francisco and his brother Ramiro had become pastors and grew to be a very strong influence for the Gospel, both in their home village as well as other villages, both Maleku and Hispanic.

Eighteen

AMOEBAS AND BUENAVISTA

Amoebas and Buenavista… strange title, you might say. What would an amoebic parasite have to do with a village called Buenavista? Not really anything, at least not directly.

Buenavista didn't have an evangelical church, and I felt a burden to go and share the gospel there. I made a plan to visit, but as time got close I cancelled. I don't remember the reason, or perhaps it was an excuse, but after this it seemed that I could never follow through.

Of course, time ticked on, as it always does.

Eventually I fell ill and went to see the doctor. After explaining my symptoms of cramps, foul breath, and weakness, the doctor was sure that I had an amoeba, a one-celled parasite which is so small that it can travel throughout the body. All the other parasites I had encountered thus far were much larger and stayed inside the digestive track.

The doctor suggested that I either go for stool tests to verify the diagnosis or take a prescription and hope for the best. I opted for the medicine, because I didn't have anywhere to stay in the city.

I took the daily dose for seven days. About ten days after that, unfortunately, the symptoms all came back. So I returned to a drugstore and got another full dose.

And again, after ten days, all the symptoms returned.

I followed the same procedure a third time, with the same end dilemma.

Around this time, I ran across an acquaintance. When I told him my problem, he said to me, "Don, you had better brace yourself, because you will have these amoebas for the rest of your life."

I noticed that he didn't mention God in our conversation. Maybe he didn't know that God has a say in our future. At any rate, I was prepared to face whatever came. However, even without medication the symptoms usually lasted three to four days at a time.

One day, while talking to Francisco after the usual Saturday night service in Tonjibe, he told me that he and a Hispanic lay preacher named Panchito were going to visit Buenavista on an evangelistic trip. Panchito had been used by God to start a number of churches; as he moved around from village to village seeking work, he would draw people together with guitar and winsome spirit, which often led to a church being started in the village.

The two men wanted to know if I would be interested in joining them to Buenavista. I said I would be more than happy, since I'd felt a burden for that village for some time already but hadn't yet been able to get there. We agreed to go the following Monday.

While making my way to El Sol the next day for the Sunday evening service, my symptoms came back in full force. It was a struggle to even make it back to El Sol.

I really felt bad, because once again I had made plans to visit Buenavista and again I wouldn't be able to go. I mopped about it for a while, but then the thought came to me that this was an attack from the adversary to deter me from going.

That's when I decided that I was going to go regardless.

It was raining the next morning, but I was determined to go. Francisco and Panchito didn't show at the given time, but even then, I was not to be deterred.

I was about one hour late getting ready to leave before the two men arrived, having been delayed due to some difficulties.

We headed down the trail together. Not much time had passed before they had gotten so far ahead that I couldn't see them. In my current condition, I just couldn't keep up. Even when they waited for me to catch up, a short time later I would have fallen behind again.

Panchito had made a homemade haversack from a large, heavy plastic bag and straps made from the inner layers of a type of bark which were fastened to the lower two corners and the neck of the bag. Well, he opened the neck of the bag and grabbed my satchel, plunking it down inside. After he fastened it back up and hoisted it onto his back, he carried on down the path.

Now I had nothing but a guitar to carry and what a difference it made! I could keep up with them now.

Eventually we came to a crick and decided to stop for a break. Francisco had brought along a large piece of cooked wild pork. He sliced off pieces for each of us and we drank the water from the crick.

As I sat there, I thought of the extra work Panchito was doing in carrying my satchel as well as his belongings. I decided that I was going to try to carry it, if possible, for a half-hour. Before we started moving again, I jumped up, grabbed the bag, and put it on my back. He, of course, tried to stop me, but I was determined to try to carry it.

I staggered all over the place as he tried to talk me into putting it back down. I kept on going, though, all the while keeping an eye on my watch. Every five minutes seemed like a half-hour.

Five minutes before the half-hour was up, something strange happened. Almost instantly, my strength returned. The straps didn't seem to cut my shoulders anymore.

I told the two brothers that I felt better now. I passed them and started walking faster. Francisco gave me competition and we walked hard for the next twenty minutes. By that time, Panchito was way out of sight behind us. I said to Francisco that we had better stop and wait for him.

When Panchito caught up with us, he asked for his bag again. I told him that I could carry it the rest of the way, but he insisted—so I gave it to him.

When we arrived at Buenavista, we made a plan to each head in different directions so we could visit different homes. Upon meeting up again we would have a service together with those who wanted to come.

The visits went extremely well, and after the small service we shared among ourselves about the opportunities we'd had to speak to the people. We were amazed at how God used us.

As for the amoebas, to this day the symptoms have never come back. God had been waiting for me to obey His voice.

Nineteen

STRETCHING OUR FAITH

Sometimes we are called to respond to situations above and beyond anything we have encountered before. That was the case during an unusually wet dry season in the lowlands.

I mentioned before that the locals cut down trees before the start of the dry season so that by the end of the dry season most of the bush would burn, leaving only the tree trunks to work around. This particular year, the rainy season never seemed to go away. We had some dry days, but then it would rain again. A single rain could set back a bush burn by two to three weeks.

As the time of the dry season seemed to pass by, the farmers became extremely concerned. If they were unable to burn, there would be no cleared land in which to plant. And if they couldn't plant, they would be out of a year's supply of food.

We decided to hold a special prayer meeting and ask God to hold off the rain long enough for the people to be able to burn their bush. This was a joint meeting of Maleku and Hispanic believers. We met in a home where everyone called on the Lord. After we had finished praying, we got up and were about leave.

Suddenly, Pedro looked up into the sky and said, "Well, it looks like it is going to rain tomorrow."

I was exasperated. "Pedro! Why would you say that? Where is your faith? We just prayed for God to hold back the rain."

I was indeed disappointed, having expected more of him than from the others.

Well, it did rain. It rained for four days, soaking the brush completely. The time of the dry season time had now passed and the expected rainy season had officially returned.

However, God in his mercy chose to honour our prayer, because the rains stopped. For more than two weeks, we had not a drop of rain. Everyone who had been vigilant burnt their bush.

And then, just as quickly, the time of grace passed and down came the rains again.

Sometime later, a very unusual event took place. Pedro's father and another villager had been out on a drinking binge. This was quite a common occurrence, and such a binge would often last two weeks or more. Pedro Sr. frequently came by his son's place when I was there and would hope to get some financial help from me by using religious language to pretend that he was interested in serving God. It was obvious that he wanted to buy more alcohol to carry on drinking. Eventually he would give up and move on.

This binge turned out differently. While Pedro Sr. and his buddy walked along a trail, he suddenly suffered an attack of some kind. He started thrashing like a madman on the ground. His buddy got scared and ran back to the village for help.

When he told the people what had happened, several of them hurried to where Pedro Sr. lay on the ground. They found him very close to the edge of the river, so that he could easily have fallen over the bank and drowned. Somehow they got him onto a homemade stretcher and with much difficulty carried him back to the village. Once there, it took three or more people to hold him to the floor of his hut.

They were at a complete loss as to what to do. One man, named Carlos, who had never once come to any of our village services, said something very strange at that point.

"Why don't you get hermano Dónal to come and casts these demons out of him?" Carlos suggested.

Pedro turned to his cousin Leonel. "Saddle up the horse and go and find him."

It was already late at night when Leonel took off on horseback to come looking for me. When he got to Margarita, somebody had informed him that they had seen me that morning heading to Tonjibe. So he carried on to Tonjibe, only to learn that I had returned to Margarita in the afternoon.

He finally found me in Margarita after midnight and told me what had happened. My first thought was that I didn't know how to help.

My second thought: is there anything my God can't handle?

I got on horseback behind Leonel and off we went. How that small horse managed to carry the both of us, I don't know!

When we arrived in El Sol, Pedro Sr. had just dropped off to sleep, probably of exhaustion. Everyone who had been sustaining Pedro Sr. went to bed, except Pedro and a woman who kept vigil at Pedro Sr.'s side while Pedro and I sat in the corridor and talked.

Pedro was in tears. "I am not right with the Lord," he said, "so how can I ask God to heal my father?"

When he described how his father had been acting, it sounded exactly like the accounts of demon possession in the Bible. We kept talking until about 3:00 a.m. when Pedro Sr. awoke.

We rushed into the room and Pedro got on the floor beside his father, holding the man's hands by his sides. He instructed me to hold his shoulders to the floor and the woman held his feet. As we held Pedro Sr. to the floor, he kept turning his head from side to side. He was grimacing and holding his lips tight together. This went on for some time until he was calm enough to lie still.

He talked to Pedro, and vice versa, but only in Malekujaica. Pedro would translate into Spanish what the man said to him.

I prayed earnestly for him. However, the attacks continued to come and go every ten to fifteen minutes. On one occasion, we relaxed a little too much and the next attack came on quicker than we could reapply our hold on him. He escaped from us and almost made it out of the house before Pedro caught him. We struggled to get him back into the room and on the floor again.

When he calmed down, he talked quite normally. He told Pedro about what had happened on the jungle trails, as well as some of the crazy thoughts that came to his mind, tempting him to do something to harm to himself. He expressed that he didn't want to serve the devil anymore; he wanted to serve Jesus.

It was strange to hear this from him.

At about eight o'clock in the morning, I believed that God was telling me to pray without ceasing. How could I do that? The only way was to pray silently.

When the next attack came on, I silently prayed for the demons to be cast out in Jesus's name. Pedro Sr. calmed down and I prayed that he would be protected from them returning. I maintained constant concentration for his protection.

He laid still for a very long time and then said to Pedro, "I feel much better now."

A while later, he asked if he could turn over on his side. After a bit of silence, I nodded to Pedro to allow it.

Pedro Sr. turned onto his side and laid still. I continued to pray.

People came in to see how he was. I only nodded in acknowledgement, then lowered my head so as not to get into any conversation with anyone.

Eventually he turned back over on this back and all was well.

By noon, he hadn't suffered a single attack in four hours. The victory was clear, and I believed God was giving me the liberty to taper off my concentration on prayer.

This poor old man was so weak after that! Before, three people could barely restrain him; now he couldn't do anything by himself. He couldn't even sit up. Every muscle in his body ached in pain. Two people had to help him to the outhouse.

He slowly recuperated his strength—and when he was able, wherever he went, he told all who would listen, "Jesus healed me." I don't think anyone of the Maleku failed to hear him say that.

Two months after the event, I saw him carrying a stalk of bananas on his shoulders. I asked him if he was back to normal and he said to me, in Spanish, "You know what? I am not back to normal yet. I am still not as strong as before and still have some muscle pain."

Regarding this whole episode, if I hadn't been ushered into this situation, I would most likely have shied away from it. In some ways, it felt like I was going through the motions. I didn't always have a lot of faith, but I knew what the Bible said I ought to do. I was certainly encouraged and blessed to see God answer prayer.

Twenty

A BULL ON THE LOOSE

One day while I was in Tonjibe, word got around that Luis's bull had broken loose from his pasture and taken off. Luis was away and his cowboy needed help to round him up again.

There were no cowboys around, only two greenhorns: myself and Francisco. We knew that bull well. He would charge at you even if you were on the other side of the fence. Neither of us could lasso a fencepost, let alone a dangerous bull, yet the cowboy gave us each a rope. We were shaking in our boots and the only thing we had was our faith in God.

We walked a long way through what was called *tacotal* (partially bushed terrain). The bush was too high to see over, so we never knew when we might suddenly come across this bull.

Suddenly, there he was in a small clearing with a clump of trees in the middle.

The cowboy instructed us to stay put while he tried to sneak up behind him, using that clump of trees as cover. I must say, this man knew his stuff. He got close enough and threw his lasso around the bull's head.

Now, an animal like this bull has a lot of strength, especially if the lasso lands around the neck and not the horns. The bull took off running, but fortunately the cowboy quickly wrapped his end of the rope around a tree.

When the bull came up short, he turned around and faced us. We didn't know what to do.

After some manoeuvring with the animal, the cowboy asked for us to bring him one of our ropes. We snuck up from the opposite side of the clearing and each passed him our rope. He then lassoed the horns of the bull, enabling him to have much better control.

The cowboy then took the third rope and threw that one over the bull's horns as well, tying it to yet another tree. With the bull secured from two sides, the cowboy got close. He had nerves of steel! He worked free the first rope that had been around the bull's neck so he could place it, as well, over the horns. He got us to tie that rope to still one other tree, which was in the opposite direction that we needed the bull to go. He then moved one rope at a time in the direction he wanted the bull to go and had us hold the ropes off to either side between the trees while he released the third rope from behind. The creature then took off in our direction but carried on past us until our ropes fetched up.

Needless to say, we were two scared greenhorns.

As we watched, the cowboy threaded one rope at a time through the trees until he was able to string it along ahead of the bull for one of us to grab hold of again. He proceeded to do the same over and over. It seemed like it would take forever to get the bull back home.

However, after we'd done this a few times, the cowboy instructed us to drop our ropes. We couldn't understand why he would say this.

"Drop your ropes," he said again.

When we finally listened, the bull trotted on towards the pasture, dragging all three ropes behind him. The cowboy had recognized when the bull was subdued and would no longer be a problem the handle.

What an experience! Francisco and I started that day as greenhorns, but we were probably a little greyer after that.

Twenty-One

OFF TO NICARAGUA

During my first mission trip, Henry and I worked primarily among the Maleku. We weren't alone in that area, though, as far as evangelical groups. But the other groups worked mostly among the Hispanics. Panchito, who I mentioned earlier, worked in connection with one of these groups. Although he had no formal Bible training, he was accepted as a lay pastor because of his record of ministry wherever he went.

But of course anyone can fail, and we know that God's earnest desire is for us to walk in his ways. When we fail, God doesn't condemn us to hell, but rather, in his mercy, he desires to restore us. He is always there to help us when we call upon him. As Ezekiel 18:23 says, *"Have I any pleasure at all that the wicked should die? saith the Lord God: and not that he should return from his ways, and live?"* Sometimes we can be harder on others than we would be on ourselves.

The story starts at a home in the Hispanic village where Panchito's church was holding a *virgilio*—an all-night service. The church had an ordained pastor in charge of their work in the area, but he had a very overbearing personality. From what I could see, he did a lot of harm while he was there.

In any case during the late-night hours, Panchito felt the need to rest, so he went to another room for a while. In the meantime, the lead pastor, for whatever reason, decided to speak out against Panchito to the rest of the church. He had assumed that Panchito was sleeping, when in reality he was awake and heard every word.

Panchito was devastated. He left the meeting and headed home, feeling very upset.

Satan likes to take advantage of such times and tempts us to do or say things we wouldn't otherwise do or say.

Panchito had been dating a woman who didn't have a very good history, although she had come to know the Lord and was very much a changed person. Distraught, Panchito went to this woman's home and moved in with her, severely damaging his testimony and the woman's own testimony. As a pastor, the reproach brought on by his actions seemed to produce eternal condemnation. I couldn't help but hear some of the talk. People appeared to be saying that there was no hope for him in heaven.

I didn't need to get involved with someone from another church, yet he was my brother so I got involved. I decided to pay him a visit.

After listening to his story, I asked, "Why don't you go and get married and fix up your testimony?"

"I can't," he replied.

"Why?"

"I don't have any papers to get married."

Then he told me about his background. He had been born along the Rio Frio, close to the Nicaraguan border. At that time, the country was predominantly Roman Catholic and no Costa Rican priests trafficked the area. Instead, a priest from Nicaragua had visited along the river and "baptized" the infants. The records Panchito would have needed likely had gone back to Nicaragua. As a result, he had no official document saying that he was Costa Rican, even though he had lived in the country all his life.

TWENTY-ONE: OFF TO NICARAGUA

He suggested that he could travel to San Carlos, Nicaragua to see if any of the Catholic churches there had a record of his birth.

I reached into my pocket and took out enough money to pay for his trip. That way, he would have no excuse to stay.

I then went on my way, but during the next week I heard more and more condemnation about Panchito. Again, I visited him and asked when he was going to leave on his trip.

He stared at me without saying anything.

"Listen," I said. "God wants you to get back up on your feet. I'll go with you, when you're ready to go."

I was convinced that God would be there to help him. Because there were so many strikes against him, I wanted to be able to testify firsthand about God's work in the midst of it.

We set a date, and after more specifics I carried on.

We had a bit of a journey getting through the jungle to reach the Rio Frio. There, we waited by the river's edge for the biweekly trip of the lancha, a cargo boat that carried produce and a few passengers down to Los Chiles and returned with another load of cargo the following day.

When it arrived, there was room for us so we climbed aboard. The heavy boat didn't travel very fast and the man guiding it steered it mostly to the centre of the river, always seeking the deepest waters. That meant that we were sitting in the direct sunlight most of the way. We often wet our arms and faces with river water to try to cool ourselves down.

On one occasion, after travelling a few hours, I took my glasses off to wet my face. When I lowered my hand back into the water, however, I accidentally knocked my glasses into the river. Oh my! I knew the boat wouldn't stop on my account, so I desperately tried to remember exactly where it had happened. Maybe I could look for them on the way back?

But I realized that the jungle looked the same everywhere. I prayed that God would help me get my glasses back.

We carried on to Los Chiles where the lancha stopped. Panchito knew a believer here who he thought would take us to San Carlos the next day. The family was very hospitable and not only offered to take us to San Carlos but provided us a place to stay.

There was one thing they wanted us to do, however, and that was to meet their son who was a pastor.

"Sure," I said without giving it much thought. "No problem."

Panchito and I had only one thought, one prayer, on our mind and that was what we had come for: to find the documents authenticating his birth.

The next day, the man from Los Chiles took us to San Carlos, Nicaragua. He waited for us on his boat while we ventured into town. Panchito had heard some disturbing stories about the priest who was in charge of church records, namely that he hadn't been very friendly.

We stopped to pray once more before proceeding farther.

As we continued up the street, we saw a man coming toward us.

"That's him," Panchito exclaimed. "That's the priest coming towards us."

How did he know? Well, the man was wearing the brown garb of a priest, for one thing!

Panchito spoke to him, telling the priest what we had come for. The priest then grumbled something about going to lunch, but turned on his heel and went back up the street.

We followed him to a small room in the church that had large shelves on three sides of the room. All the shelves were full of very big books.

"What's your father's name?" the priest asked gruffly.

When Panchito told him, the man walked around looking at the backs of the books. He pulled out one of them and plunked it down on the table in the centre of the room. He opened the book and, after a quick look, closed it.

"It's not there."

He returned the book to the shelf and headed for the door. At the doorway, he stopped short, though, and turned around.

"What's your mother's name?"

He must have just remembered that some children, when there was no known father, were listed under their mother's name. Panchito answered him, and again the priest walked around until he spotted a certain book.

After flipping through the pages, he exclaimed, "There it is."

TWENTY-ONE: OFF TO NICARAGUA

The priest opened a drawer and took out a yellowish pad and wrote the information on the top sheet. He tore off the top sheet and gave it to Panchito.

Upon returning the book, he left the room without saying goodbye. We were too elated to think about that because we had that precious piece of paper in our hands!

As we headed down the street, Panchito said that we needed to go right away to the representative of the municipality, to get him to issue a birth certificate, on the basis of the *fé de bautismo* paper we now had.

This man apparently owned a restaurant, so we went there to ask for him. The people we met there, however, weren't sure if the man was around. After all, it was Saturday—the day he usually went to his farm.

Surprisingly, on this particular Saturday he *was* there. When he arrived, he introduced himself and asked us to sit down with him at one of the tables. He called a woman over and gave her our paper, then asked her to unlock his office and go in and prepare a birth certificate.

He also had the restaurant prepare dinner for all three of us.

As we were finishing our meal, the woman returned with the certificate ready for him to sign.

Wow! Talk about the hand of God! Who can deny that? We were treated like special guests. As David said in Psalm 23:5, *"You prepare a table before me in the presence of my enemies"* (NKJV). The enemy was in the obstacles and in the people who didn't think God would forgive this man.

We got back to Los Chiles and straightaway were reminded of our agreement to meet the son of the man from Los Chiles. Even though I was anxious to get back, we couldn't turn him down. How could we not fulfill his wish when we were so over the moon with God's provision?

We decided to visit the man's son the next day. I hoped the visit wouldn't take more than half a day.

In the morning, we headed out on a trail and soon came to Medio Queso river. There was a narrow flat-bottomed boat for us to cross with. However, this boat was very *celóso* (jealous). If we moved slightly to one side, it would tip suddenly; if we then overreacted the other way, we might well tip right over into the river. I think this boat didn't want to take us across and would have rather dumped us over.

I must say, I was rather surprised when we made it to the other side still dry.

We walked for some time before coming to a farm where we were told to wait. We waited quite a while in the heat of the day, and I began to wonder where this young man, this pastor, might be.

I finally asked someone what we were waiting for.

"We are waiting for the horses."

"Horses!" I said. "What do we need horses for?"

"Oh, we have a long way to go yet. We will go the rest of the way by horseback."

So much for a half-day excursion! Reality had begun to sink in and I wondered just what we had gotten ourselves in for.

As night closed in, we arrived on horseback at the village of Isla Chica—meaning "Small Island," although I couldn't figure out why it was called an island. All the houses in this quaint little village were thatched with palm leaves.

We met the pastor, who was very glad to meet us and immediately asked me to deliver the message for the church's evening service. He didn't know me, but perhaps he confided in us so completely because we were accompanied by his parents. He never asked any questions.

The service went very well. I don't remember what I spoke on, but after I sat down the pastor gave an invitation and two people accepted the Lord as their Saviour, praise the Lord. The trip was worth it all, and this considerably calmed my anxiety about getting back.

However, I was still bent on leaving at five o'clock in the morning.

We were up bright and early, but the horses couldn't be found anywhere. We learned that the horses had been left loose in order to graze, since there weren't any fenced-off pastures in this relatively new village. The villagers began to assume that the horses had ventured back by themselves.

We braced ourselves for a long walk, but at nine o'clock someone spotted the horses in a nearby alcove, allowing us to breathe a definite sigh of relief.

TWENTY-ONE: OFF TO NICARAGUA

We headed out and eventually made it back to Los Chiles by nightfall.

The lancha didn't have a trip scheduled back upriver the next day, so I asked the boat driver if I could borrow a boat to go back upriver to have a look for my glasses—and he readily agreed to this.

It was a two-hour ride upriver to where I believed my glasses had gone overboard. We anchored the boat above the expected place, and Panchito kept watch while I jumped into the water armed with only a facemask.

I dove into the depths and scanned the river bottom as the current carried me downstream. After arriving a considerable distance downstream, I would be forced to return to the surface and swim or wade along the river's edge until I got back to the boat. Then I would repeat the process.

I did this for two hours, to no avail. By that time I was exhausted and shivering cold. At least I had given it an earnest effort.

Still, I believed that God was going to return my glasses by some other means.

We returned to Los Chiles to spend the night, then took the lancha the next day to return home.

Panchito lost no time in getting legally married after we returned.

Around this time, I took a trip to the city and picked up my mail, which contained a letter with a cheque for $115. The money represented a portion of an inheritance that had been given to me. God, I believed, had supplied me with the money so I could buy a new pair of glasses.

I went to an optometrist in San José, who told me to have a seat. Fifteen minutes later, the staff asked me to come in to have my eyes examined. Afterwards they used a machine to determine the lens I needed.

I expected to be told when to come back at a later time. Instead I was asked again to have a seat. Maybe ten or fifteen minutes later, the optometrist asked me come have my glasses fitted.

Shortly after, I walked out of there wearing a new pair of glasses with an up-to-date prescription. That was almost unbelievable for me—and the money I had received in the mail had paid for it all.

God's provision was better than I had asked. My eyes had changed sufficiently that I had needed a new prescription anyway.

This reminded me of Ephesians 3:20: *"Now to Him who is able to do exceedingly abundantly above all that we ask or think, according to the power that works in us..."* (NKJV)

Twenty-Two

CAYUCO GOES MISSING

One day when I arrived in El Sol, I came to the river's edge and found that there was no cayuco (dugout canoe) to cross with. The one I usually crossed with was locked up and no one was allowed to use it.

I didn't think much of it at the time. I just removed my footwear, rolled up my pant legs, and waded across. If there had been more rain at the time, crossing the river would have been much more of a challenge.

The river ran through the centre of the village and there was no easy way to access the village from the other side if a person was coming from Margarita.

The house where we always held services was, of course, on the other side. Over the years, they had placed fallen trees across the river to serve as bridges, but in heavy rains the river would overflow its banks and the tree trunks would float away.

When I reached the other side and made my way to Leonel's place, his wife informed me of a conversation she'd had with Elíjio, the owner of the dugout canoe. She had asked him if I could use it.

Elíjio's response? "No. Nobody can use it."

She had pushed the issue a little further, or maybe a lot further. "You're not going to allow a man of God to use it?"

Remember that this is the same man who had possibly saved my life a few years earlier, and who had defended me in front of a rude stranger who hadn't thought I was one of them.

But his answer was the same: "No."

On hearing of this conversation, I right away thought that God would respond to this.

Two weeks went by, and then a heavy rain hit. The river came up and overflowed its banks. The canoe and the stake holding it disappeared, and Elíjio went looking all up and down both sides of the river, all the way to where the river emptied into the Rio Frio. He couldn't find his boat. If it had made it to the big river, then there wasn't much chance of it ever being found.

When I came back to the village after that incident, the villagers wasted no time in telling me about the lost canoe and Elíjio's vain attempts to try finding it.

I decided that it was time to pay a visit to Elíjio.

On my way to his house, God put a message in my mind.

When I entered his house and sat down, I listened for quite some time to his story of the vain attempt to locate his boat.

"Elíjio," I said when he had finished, "by the grace of God, if you look straight over there behind those bushes, I think you will find your boat."

I pointed across the river, across a clearing, to some bushes that didn't yet rise to the full height of the jungle. I had no way of knowing for sure that the boat would be there, but I believe God directed me to say that to him.

Elíjio just looked across the way and said nothing. I got up and left.

A week later, as I approached the village again, there was a lot of excitement. Everyone was telling me that Elíjio had found his canoe.

"Well, do you think I can use it to cross the river?" I asked.

"Oh yes, you can use it."

I believe God did that for all the villagers. Sadly, I must say that, to my knowledge, despite all that God had revealed to Elíjio, he did not repent of his ways and died as a relatively young man. God had spoken loudly in this village to a number of people, as he also did in the other palenques. God loved these people and wanted to draw them unto himself.

Twenty-Three

MAKING A DUGOUT CANOE

I decided that I should make a dugout canoe to enable me to get around the rivers, so I inquired about how to go about doing that.

The first thing I needed was a large cedar tree. The next thing, which was critical, was to be able to fell that tree without splitting the trunk.

Pedro and Leonel found me a suitable tree, and I successfully accomplished the first two criteria. We measured a forty-foot chunk of the trunk, which would be suitable for making a canoe.

I got in touch with a craftsman who would make it into a dugout canoe, but he told me to first remove most of the excess wood with my chainsaw, which would speed up his part of the job considerably. Not only was I able to shape the boat from the outside, I was also able to remove a lot of the excess wood from the inside.

Then the craftsman went to work with his tools. I was a little surprised by what he did. After smoothing and shaping the outside, he proceeded to drill holes in the shell from stem to stern. He explained that this was necessary in order to get a uniform thickness all over. He explained that afterwards he would make special plugs to fill each hole so there wouldn't be any leaks.

As the boat neared completion, people came by to admire it.

In particular, Charía had been eyeing the progress closely. He had often suggested to me that we go hunting and fishing together, and instead of using the Spanish word for whatever we might catch he would use the Malekujaica words. I could never tell for sure whether he was serious.

When the boat was finished, though, he asked me again and I was determined to find out for sure by calling his bluff—if that's what it was. But it turned out that he was serious and he and Nicanor soon made a plan to go with me on my first real boat fishing trip. I didn't know what it would be like.

On the day, we got our stuff together and headed down the small El Sol River until it emptied into the much larger Rio Frio. The long dugout was easier to manoeuvre in the bigger river. One person could fish from the bow as we travelled downstream and moved along mostly by the current, although someone always sat at the stern with a paddle to govern our direction. There were large catfish to be caught by throwing a fishing line from the bow ahead of the boat.

Going downstream wasn't very difficult because the river moved relatively slowly. We did have to watch for fallen trees in the river. Once in a while we'd see crocodiles sunning themselves on the riverbanks, though. We only needed to use the polling stick occasionally, on the downriver trip, to help manoeuvre in tight spots, usually due to debris in the river. And sometimes Charía and Nicanor would stop and go hunting in the jungle before wanting to continue on down the river.

When mealtime came, they would pull over to the side of the river and start a fire to cook some of their catch.

In the late afternoon, we stopped for the night in a place where they had camped before. The Maleku knew where these places were.

After we'd eaten supper and the meat was set up on sticks above the fire to smoke and dry over night, we stretched out under the lean-to, which was only wide enough to cover about half of each of us. It might protect our upper body from the dew but it didn't protect any part of us from the hoards of mosquitoes that buzzed around at night!

These trips usually took place during the dry season, so rain normally wasn't a factor. There were two things in particular we had to contend with: heat and mosquitoes. One of these at a time would have been much easier to deal with. If it had been cooler, I could have covered my head. If there had been fewer mosquitoes, I could have brought half my blanket up to my waist and used the other half to chase the bugs away.

For me, the mosquitoes never got the message to stay away for a bit. With one quick swipe with one hand, I would catch a dozen mosquitoes. I'd try covering my head, but I couldn't stand the heat. I feared that if I tried the half-blanket method again, and if I remained that way, I would have no blood left by morning.

At one point, I even got up and started wandering around in the dark to try and pass the time.

When day began to break, the agony was finally over. But I was concerned about how long the trip was going to last. Charía and Nicanor hadn't told me yet.

After breakfast but before we got ready to go, Charía announced that we were going back upriver. Really! I was surprised, but at the same time I wondered how I would have endured the mosquitoes if the trip had lasted for several days. I didn't say anything, nor did he say why we were going back so soon.

I mentioned something about the mosquitoes, but he didn't offer to confirm whether the night's plague of mosquitoes had anything to do with it. At least we all agreed that sleeping in the jungle would be a lot more comfortable if we had mosquito netting. This made me think that the mosquitoes may have affected them more than they let on.

Anyway, I hoped that I wasn't the cause of their decision to return. I had at least won their appreciation for shooting iguanas.

The return journey was a much different process. One person had to be at the bow of the boat to poll it upstream while another paddled from the stern, guiding the boat. We didn't do any more fishing, and, due to the strenuous work involved, the third person got to take rests.

Once we got back, it was time to rest our aching bodies, the arms and shoulders especially, and talk about the trip.

A few days after, I went out to the city and, amongst other things, picked up some mosquito netting. When I later talked to Charía, I mentioned my purchase, to kind of test the waters. I was hoping he might be game to invite me again sometime in the future. Which he did, right away. I decided to take him up on it, pleased to know that I hadn't put him off on the last trip.

However, he mentioned right away that this next trip would be eight days long and we would be hunting turtles. I had no idea how they would get the turtles.

I also assumed they must have purchased mosquito netting of their own, seeing as they had thought it was such a good idea.

When the day came to head out again in the new dugout, I saw that Leonel's mother—who was also Charía's sister—was coming with us. We got our stuff in the boat, including three large nets.

We started fishing as soon as we were on the Rio Frio. I soon found out what kind of skill this woman had at fishing. We stopped at small inlet to catch a different kind of fish and she had little trouble bringing them in. I was at the other end of the boat, having no luck at all. If I did get a bite, it wouldn't seem to get caught on my hook. Whenever she saw me pull my rod out without a catch, she'd say, "You let him get away." I would instead argue that the fish had jumped off my hook.

This went on for some time, and finally she suggested that we switch places. I thought this might help me catch some fish, but to my disappointment I still couldn't land any. And to make me feel even worse, she continued to haul in fish where I had been convinced there weren't any.

Feeling a little perturbed, I grabbed the rod firmly with both hands. When I felt a nibble, I yanked my rod back as fast as I could. Not only did I not get a fish, but the hook even straightened out some. Maybe I had hooked a log rather than a fish…

I figured I had better rest easy and accept that this was one thing I wasn't good at and let her have her little joke.

TWENTY-THREE: MAKING A DUGOUT CANOE

We continued downriver until it was time to stop for night. They again picked a former campground and built a fire. I got out my netting and asked them where they were going to string up their mosquito netting.

"We don't have any," Charía answered.

I was dumbfounded. After all, they'd told me they were ready for this trip and the netting wasn't expensive.

"Why?" I asked.

"We don't need any."

Now I was convinced that I was the reason they had returned early last time, but they wouldn't say a word to me about it.

I proceeded to string up my netting over a fresh bunch of soft branches. I crawled under the net and peeled down to my waist. As I lay there and listened to the *flip-flop*, *flip-flop* of their blankets, I couldn't help but go to sleep with a silent chuckle on my face.

For the next four days, we travelled downriver, fishing and hunting as we went, until we reached Caño Negro. As we got close, we started to see the heads of turtles sticking up above the surface of the water. There were thousands of them. But when we approached, they disappeared. When I looked behind us, though, they would reappear.

On our way down, we had met another boat with Maleku from another palenque, which I thought was quite a coincidence. However, at Caño Negro we encountered a number of boats steered by Maleku. To my surprise, they had planned this trip before I had ever asked to come along. By making a plan with me, it had meant they could bring an extra boat load.

I was, without a doubt, learning something new at every turn.

But how were they going to catch these turtles? They most definitely had a plan. Some went on ahead downriver. Then the others got out a long net that was about six feet wide but long enough to reach across the river. A group of people held each end and proceeded to drag it down the river. The turtles were literally herded by the net—although if a turtle dove deep enough, it could swim under the net and escape.

The rest of us followed behind the net in our boats.

As we came to a small inlet, I noticed that the people who had gone on ahead were spread out across the river, splashing and making noises to discourage the turtles from swimming further downstream.

Meanwhile, the group holding the net on the opposite side of the river moved across to close off the inlet. Both groups moved along the sides of the inlet until the water was so shallow that the net touched the bottom, leaving no room for the turtles to escape.

Now everyone moved into the corralled area with their boats and started grabbing turtles and placing them in the nets they had brought. There was great excitement! Since these were snaping turtles, every once in a while someone got bit and let out a scream while the others burst into laughter. It was mayhem until the nets were all full, the boats so loaded that they couldn't carry anymore.

Our own dugout was so loaded down that the water came up to two inches from the edge of the boat. Needless to say, we didn't want to rock the boat when it was that full.

I can honestly say, I had never seen so much excitement among the Maleku before. It was an experience to remember.

We now headed back upriver, but instead of travelling together everyone spread out, as they must have done on the way down, stopping at different campsites at night. Every once in a while during the journey we would hear a speed boat or the cargo boat approaching. We would have to quickly get close to the side of the river and turn the boat perpendicular to the wake. One wave, side on, could sink our craft. Even still, each passing wave still dumped water into our boat from both sides. We had to bail it out after the waves settled.

We polled and paddled until it was time to stop for night. By that time, we very sore and tired and I wondered if I was going to be able to function at all the next day. But after a night's rest, we would be up again at five, still very sore. Much to my surprise, though, after a bit of workout the pain would subside and I would be able to do my part.

What a relief it was to relax when we finally made it back to El Sol the following day!

But what did the villagers do with all those turtles, you might ask? Turtles can be kept alive in nets for one month, as long as they're sprinkled with water every day or so, especially on hot days.

Turtles are a good source of meat, although a person must be careful at first about eating turtle meat. The very first time I ate turtle, I knew nothing of any problems with them. The meat tasted good and I might have mistaken it for beef. I happened to be given turtle meat one day and I didn't think anything of it.

About two days later, while visiting at a Hispanic man's house, I felt severe cramps come on. He asked what I had eaten and I assured him that I hadn't eaten anything out of the ordinary. He knew that it was the time of the year when Maleku hunt turtles, though, so he asked me if I had eaten any turtle meat.

"Well, not recently," I said. "Maybe two or more days ago I had some."

"That's it. That's what has caused your cramps," he told me. "Turtle meat is very hard to digest. It takes time to adjust to eating it."

He gave me a large glass of sour orange juice.

I made my way up to another house, but I was in much pain that I stopped there. They homeowner gave me some milk of magnesia tablets and got me to rest on a canvas bed. I fell asleep, but when I awoke I was fine.

I never had another recurrence of that experience, even though I've eaten turtle meat many times since.

Twenty-Four

A DIFFERENT WAY TO GUATUSO

I knew there must be another way to get into the palenques from Ciudad Quesada other than flying, but I didn't know how. I decided to venture to find it.

I took a bus to La Fortuna from Ciudad Quesada, which was about a two-hour journey. I ate dinner in this beautiful little town at the foot of the Arenal volcano. The people of La Fortuna, which means "the fortunate," were indeed fortunate when the volcano erupted. It blew off partly down from the peak, on the other side, and the wind carried the ash in the opposite direction from the town.

Three villages on the other side were seriously affected and close to a hundred people died. Roofs caved in from the weight of the ash and the immediate area was covered by as much as two feet. The ashfall was quite noticeable sixty miles away.

This serious eruption happened between the time of my first two-week trip with Henry and my first long stay in the country. Although the volcano remained active after that, with smaller eruptions occurring for the next forty years, the next most serious event happened in 2010. From the pictures I've seen, it produced a new crater a little higher up from the old one.

After walking along a road for a mile or two, I headed out on a trail that, I was told, would take me to El Venado, and from there to the palenques and Guatuso. A number of trails branched out to other places. Every time I passed anyone, I would ask if I was on the right trail for El Venado. After assuring me that it was, they would usually caution me about another split farther on and advise me which one to take. Other times I would have to orient myself with only the help of the cone of the volcano, visible over the trees.

After making one particular guess and walking for a while without meeting anyone, I stopped at a farmhouse. There was a small dog barking, which didn't worry me too much.

"Good afternoon," I called.

Suddenly, the sound of my voice aroused a large dog which charged at me full speed. A woman shouted for him to stop, which didn't seem to make any difference.

From childhood, I knew that the worst thing I could do was run. So I stood still as a soldier standing at attention while two dogs circled me. The larger one growled and gnashed his teeth against my balled-up fists. He seemed as though he wanted to bite me, but finally the dogs obeyed the woman's voice and left me alone.

When I asked whether I was on the right trail, it again turned out to be the correct one and she told me about the next split and which path to take. I thanked her and carried on—still in one piece, thankfully.

I hadn't realized how long it would take to get to El Venado and darkness was quickly approaching. I carried on, believing that God would somehow supply me with a place to stay for the night. But it soon got so dark that I couldn't see the trail very well anymore… and I walked straight over a bank and fell down.

I rested for a bit and snacked on a can of juice and cookies I had bought in La Fortuna. When I got up and started walking again, I moved slower than before and paid better attention to where I was going in the dark.

TWENTY-FOUR: A DIFFERENT WAY TO GUATUSO

In the distance, I heard some singing, which I thought must be coming from some drunkards as the sound seemed quite distorted.

As I got closer, though, the sound improved and I soon recognized that the songs were hymns. I passed by the house where people were singing and came to a river. However, I couldn't get across because it had strong current and was quite deep.

I went back to the house, intending to ask the people how to get across the river. They told me that I would find a bridge farther up the river.

Then they asked me where I was going to stop for night, to which I answered that I didn't know yet. They invited me to stay there for night and to join them in their church service. I was more than pleased to do that.

After the service had finished, the household's mother explained that all of her children had accepted the Lord as their Saviour except for one boy, whom she pointed out to me. I took him to one side and talked to him. I don't remember everything I said, but I shared the gospel, but I later found out that the boy had expressed a desire to travel with me some time. I am disappointed that the opportunity never came about.

The family got some food ready for me from their leftovers. I remember that they served me a pile of *plátanos* (plantains), a full pot of coffee, and a glass of milk. I ate the plantains and drank all the coffee and milk, yet it didn't totally quench my thirst. I needed to ask for a glass of water as well.

At last they supplied me with a canvas bed to sleep on. What a luxury! I slept well and got up at six o'clock and had breakfast. After saying good bye, I headed down the trail.

By midday I had arrived at Tonjibe. It was hard to believe that the whole distance from Ciudad Quesada to Tonjibe, a couple of hours short of Guatuso, had taken me a day and a half, yet only it took twenty minutes by air. However, by flying I was missing out on so much adventure—remembering, of course, that the adventure could be dangerous too.

The greater benefit was the opportunity to meet and talk with more people.

Arenal volcano

Twenty-Five

MY FOURTH TRIP SOUTH
Fall 1974

When I left Costa Rica the third time, I expected that I would return. I believed that God had used Henry, Anne, and myself to establish a foothold for the gospel among the Maleku. I had gained a lot of respect in all three palenques, but God had worked in a special way while I followed through with what Scripture tells us to do. I saw God's hand at work, not that I had a lot of faith.

I felt like these people had become part of me, yet I had a difficult lesson to learn about where to go next in my ministry. I saw two things happening. People were increasingly growing dependent on me, which didn't always translate into a greater dependence on God. This meant that my helping hand being taken for granted by some.

Henry and I once had a discussion on this topic.

"We need to trust the believers to the Holy Spirit," he told me.

I must say that I disagreed. How could I let go of family, which is what they had become to me?

However, in support of his way of thinking, if an adult always walks alongside young children as they learn to walk, will they ever gain the confidence to walk by themselves?

Spiritually, believers need to learn to lean on God. This is a hard lesson, and many of us never become very successful at doing it. Or we stray from continuing along the path.

After I returned to Canada the second time, I very quickly began making plans to go back. When I saw an old Rambler for sale, the price was right, so I bought it. From my newfound mechanical experience, I decided to overhaul the motor. Although if I had known what I found out later, I would have looked for another second-hand motor—or, better still, left the car parked in the field where I first spotted it.

By the school of hard knocks, I had learned how to check all the major moving parts of a motor once it was taken apart. I dismantled this motor six times before I managed to remedy most of its ills.

The first time I replaced the piston rings, the second time the rod bearings, the third time the main bearings, and then the cam bearings, the piston wrist pins, and the oil pump. All this could have been done at once. However, the experience I gathered served me well in the years to come. Getting reliable mechanic work done on the mission field can be challenging.

As I prepared to return, I thought of how I might meet my future needs. I bought a school bus that had been taken out of service, thinking that if I sold it in Central America, where many were used for public service, the proceeds could help me financially.

I should have just trusted God for my provision.

The first step was to strip down the motor. I noticed some scoring on the crank shaft. My cousin, who was a mechanic, suggested that I get it turned at a machine shop and to install oversized bearings. That sounded like it would cost more money than I could spare, so I decided to shim the bearings until they came in specs with plastigage.[4] I then put the motor back together.

---

4 Plastigage is a clay-like thread that, when placed in the bearings and tightened in place, will flatten to tell the mechanic how much clearance there is.

TWENTY-FIVE: MY FOURTH TRIP SOUTH

I finally had both the Rambler and the bus in order. Or at least, so I thought. Now I needed a hitch to tow the Rambler behind the bus. My uncle had welding gear and had told me that I could help myself if I wanted to build a hitch. He had taught himself to weld, so he figured I could do the same.

I got some old bedframes for angle iron and went to work. The welding job didn't look the best, but I hoped above all else that it would be strong. I may have used two or three times as many rods as an experienced welder might have used, but it did hold together well. Later, when I was travelling in the U.S., twice I had to brake hard to avoid what easily could have been an accident; the hitch showed no sign of strain.

As I prepared to go, people who never went to church or seemed to take any interest in the gospel gave me gifts. I think it's because the idea of my undertaking had left an impression. However, in hindsight, I would have sooner left with my usual handbag and maybe a small suitcase.

Henry and his family had gone back down south again as well, but instead of returning to Costa Rica they had gone to Belize where there was a Mennonite colony. They had hoped to help with an evangelical Mennonite church there.

When they left Canada, they had wanted to take more luggage with them, but they hadn't been able to find enough space in their vehicle. So when Henry heard that I was coming south with a bus, he suggested that I pick up their left-behind luggage and bring it to him in Belize on my way to Costa Rica. That was about a thousand miles out of my way, but I was indeed indebted to the Teigrob family for all they had done for me.

After I got on the road, I picked up some important bus-driving skills. I had never driven a vehicle with that many gears before!

I picked up the Teigrobs' luggage and put it under the seats, as there was lots of room.

When I arrived at the U.S. border, the immigration official asked me where I was going and if I would be leaving the bus in the States. I told him that this wasn't my plan. He barely glanced at my Canadian passport and wished me a safe trip.

Later on, in Pennsylvania, I got into a bit of a muddle. There was a detour that led me off the four-lane highway onto a narrow, twisty two-lane road. After at least twenty miles, I entered a freeway and headed south. I was happy to be on the freeway, especially since it was night-time.

But I was only on it for about a half-hour when I saw a sign ahead: "Freeway ends. All traffic must exit." I came to the end of the ramp and could exit either north or south. I wanted to go south, so I turned right to follow the two-lane highway south. I travelled for quite a while until I saw yet another sign directing me to the same freeway! I assumed they must have recently completed another piece of this highway.

Once again, I was happy to be back on the four-lane highway. I travelled for a while before my headlights revealed a bank ahead that looked very much like a bank I had seen before. Now I became very alert, trying to see if I would recognize anything else.

I was quite sure that I did.

Now I guessed that, very soon, I would come upon the sign saying, "Freeway ends. All traffic must exit." Sure enough, I came off onto the same ramp as before.

This time I chose to follow the two-lane highway north, even though I didn't want to go north. I travelled for a while until I became so concerned about my whereabouts that I decided to pull over to study my five-year-old Pennsylvania map.

While I was stopped, a car pulled up by my left driver's window and stopped. We opened our corresponding windows and the driver asked me if I had a problem.

"Yes, I do have a problem," I said. "I'm lost."

With that, he backed up until he could pull in behind me. Then he lit up two flares and set them on the side of the road. He came up the other side and stepped into the bus. He explained that he was an off-duty policeman and would try to help. I gave him my map and asked him to show me on the map where I was located, so I could get onto the freeway heading south.

He studied the map for a while.

"I can't figure out your map either," he said after a while. "But I can tell you how to get where you want to go."

His directions were simple. I was to continue on until I came to the next set of traffic lights, then turn left. At the following set of traffic lights, I was to turn left again, which would take me straight onto the freeway.

Sure enough, it did.

I believe God that got put this man in my path at the right time to help me. I looked at my map again later, but no map could reveal to me where I had gone wrong that night.

It was the beginning of December when I had left Nova Scotia, and I had hoped to get far enough south to avoid running into a snowstorm and ultimately reach Belize before Christmas.

As I travelled down through Virginia, though, the snow started to fall. I wanted to keep going, hoping to outdrive the snow.

It was dark before I reached Tennessee, a state in which they were still in the process of building a few of their freeways. The two-lane highway I had to travel along was loaded with traffic, and most of it seemed to consist of trucks. I had never seen so many trucks! Although I had tried to drive as close to the speed limit as I could on the narrow road, the truck drivers seemed to always want to go faster. If I let a few trucks go by me, there would be, in no time, another dozen or more of trucks lined up behind me.

The precipitation had changed from snow to rain by this point. Since I was very tired, I eagerly looked for a place to stop.

Finally, I spotted what looked like a trucker's layby. I quickly pulled in and parked beside a big truck which shielded me from the blasts of air being generated by the passing traffic. Although I had the noise of diesel motors running around me, I soon dropped off to sleep.

The next day went quite well and it wasn't long before I was back on a four-lane highway.

But at nightfall, the headlights suddenly went out. The problem was due to power not getting to the headlights. I thought it should be an easy fix, considering my background, but I had to pray about this for some time before I could resolve the issue.

Sometime later, the transmission started to slip out of the second to last gear. This wasn't a big concern for me right then, but I was concerned for the future when I would have hills or mountains to contend with. While travelling in the southern states and on four-lane highways, I only needed to hold the gearshift in place for short intervals while moving up into the top gear. I never needed to remain in that gear for very long.

I finally arrived at the Mexican border, expecting some difficulty but not as much as I got. The immigration officer told me that one driver couldn't take two licenced vehicles into the country. I couldn't believe this to be true and wondered if it was just a policy at that particular crossing.

I went back into the U.S. and travelled westward along the border until I came to the next crossing. Again, they told me the same thing. At this point, I accepted that it must be an official ruling and I had no choice but to return to the U.S. and think over my next move.

It was between 7:30 and 8:00 in the morning when I made my attempt to head back over into the U.S. To do so, I needed to cross over four lanes. At a break in the boulevard, I tried to merge into heavy traffic, but no one wanted to let me in. Now I was also blocking traffic heading south into Mexico.

I sat there for a while until a driver, about three cars back, gave me the signal that he was going to let me in. When the traffic cleared in front of him, I pulled in but needed two lanes to swing my long train around the boulevard. No one wanted to give me the space I needed, and the impatient drivers behind the courteous one were upset and started blowing their horns.

It was madness. With the heavy traffic merging from six lanes into four, two cars tried to merge into the lane I needed at the same time. They got so close to each other that they hooked bumpers. As I watched, they jumped out and started yelling at each other.

Traffic cleared in front of them!

"Thank you, Lord," I said as I finally pulled in and continued back over into the U.S.

What would I do next? It was almost Christmas and I couldn't get into Mexico. I found a place to park so I could take some time to think and pray.

The Lord knows the way through the wilderness, I said to myself. *And all I have to do is follow.*

The next day was Sunday and I wanted to attend a service. I found a church that might be suitable, but their service was almost finished already when I arrived. I decided to wait until the people came out so I could talk to someone.

However, as the people exited the building I saw a number of them quickly light up cigarettes—and many of the women were dressed in very short skirts. I decided that this wasn't what I was looking for.

I carried on walking down the street and came to a house with cars in the yard with bumper stickers saying "Jesus Saves." I decided to knock on their door. When a guy came to the door, I told him briefly who I was and what I was trying to do. He told me of some other people who were doing mission work in Mexico and suggested that I talk with them.

I thanked him and followed his directions to this other person's house. I knocked on their door and again offered a brief explanation of who I was and the dilemma I found myself in.

"We are just setting down to dinner," the man said. "Why don't you come in and join us?"

He introduced me to his family and bade me to sit down with them. After he prayed, he told me that they had just came back from a mission trip in Mexico and their V8 station wagon was in very poor shape. They were fortunate to have made it back home.

I told him that I had a problem with the transmission on the school bus as well.

"Well," he said, "if you would like to help my son repair our car, he could also help you with the bus."

"But it's almost Christmas and I don't want to interfere with your plans…"

"You will not be interfering with any plans. Besides you can join us in the services we're having in a border town in Mexico. It will be a joy for us to have you."

Wow! I was a stranger and they took me in. This reminded me of what it says in Matthew 25:35: *"For I was hungry and you gave Me food; I was thirsty and you gave Me drink; I was a stranger and you took Me in…"* (NKJV)

The next day, we went to work on the family's station wagon and pulled the engine apart. Five of the eight pistons were cracked, which this man blamed on the poor grade of gas in Mexico. A lot has changed in this regard in the years since then! We installed new pistons and reassembled the engine.

This was the first time I had spent Christmas away from anyone I knew and it felt quite lonely, but these people did their best to make me feel like part of their family. I enjoyed going with them for the services across the border.

After Christmas, we decided to tackle my transmission. This transmission was really designed for a truck and we needed a winch cable to lower it to the ground. Then we dragged it out from under the bus.

Transmission repair wasn't a job I had any experience with, but since I couldn't afford to take it to a shop we pulled it apart. The shifting apparatus seemed to be in good shape, with no sign of wear. We noticed, though, that a main shaft and a pilot shaft, which were coupled together in the middle, had a lot of slack between them.

We took out both shafts and brought them to a machine shop. The machinist said that the main shaft could be built up, but the much smaller pilot shaft would be difficult to repair and wouldn't be very expensive to buy new. The total cost of the repair was only a little over $100.

When we had the repair done, we put the transmission back together and hoisted it into place. However, when we tried driving the bus it acted like it was in gear the whole time. We pulled off the gear shift cover and could see that it was shifting the gears fine.

Then it occurred to me that the machinist had said he hadn't known how much he should build up the main shaft. Maybe he had built it up a thousandth of an inch too much.

"Lord, by faith we have done the best we knew how," I prayed alongside the two men helping me. "Let it be according to your will concerning this transmission."

TWENTY-FIVE: MY FOURTH TRIP SOUTH

I got in the driver's seat and started up the bus with the brake applied. I put it in first gear and released the brake and clutch. I shoved it into second, then third, and on up through the gears as the vehicle picked up speed. I drove it around for a while.

I never had any other problems with it, and the transmission never slipped out of gear again, praise the Lord.

I found a place where I could park the bus for an extended period of time and planned instead to get to Belize by car.

By this time, the first of January had come and gone and I decided to call Henry in Belize to tell him where I was. He was quite anxious to hear from me and had been wondering where I had gotten to. I might add that the phone call wasn't only expensive but there was only one phone in the village where he was staying. I had to make one call to get someone to fetch him, then hope that he would be there when I called a second time.

Henry surprised me with some of his own plans. He wanted me to wait where I was until he could fly up to meet me. He suggested that we travel together around the southern U.S. with my Rambler to look for an airplane to take to Belize.

We spent the next number of days searching for a plane that would suit his budget. When we eventually found one, he flew it down to Weslaco, Texas. The Missionary Aviation Fellowship (MAF) had a hangar there and could help to get some needed work done on it before it could be flown to Belize.

Henry wasn't keen on getting involved in driving the bus to Belize, so he and I went by car to Belize with the plan of returning later; he would get the plane and I would pick up the bus.

The trip to Belize went quite well, except for one sudden event near the end. After entering Belize, Henry said that he would drive because he knew the roads better than I did and it was now night-time. At about 1:00 a.m., we had gotten to within five miles of our destination, a village called Blue Creek. I was dozing in the passenger's seat when suddenly the car plunged into a river.

Needless to say, I woke up with a start, wondering what was going on. Henry, in a rush to arrive, had forgotten about a river that crossed the road. The river wasn't very deep, but the splash had killed the engine.

Instead of getting out, he just settled back in his seat and said, "It's my turn to sleep now."

I wondered if he had been sleeping already.

The nerve! I had to get out and try to dry off the sparkplug wires and the distributor to get the car running again. Eventually, I got it going and we were able to drive out of the river and on to Blue Creek.

I was already rethinking some of the events of the trip, considering all the obstacles I'd faced on the way. I thought about what God was saying in all this. My destination was Costa Rica, but now I was in Belize—and it seemed as though I would be here for a while at least.

The Lord knows the way through the wilderness and all I have to do is follow, I reminded myself.

But was I following, or had I been running ahead of the Lord with the whole idea of bringing the bus down? The church that had supported me last time was no longer supporting me over a precise doctrinal disagreement.

Then came a question to my mind: had not God provided for me at the Texas border with a family who had some slight differences in doctrine? This, to me, was an example of God working where the rubber grips the road, so to speak. We worked together physically to meet each other's needs and we worked together spiritually in the services we attended in Mexico.

But then, why was I hindered from getting back to Costa Rica? Was Henry right about needing to trust believers to the Holy Spirit? Having laboured with tears to get a church started in each of the palenques, what if, after such birth pains, it all came to nothing?

Then came another question: whose church was it, ours or God's? And if God was leading me to Belize, he must be able to take care of his church in Costa Rica.

Twenty-Six

BACK FOR THE BUS

Two months later, I returned to Texas for the bus. My plan now was to drive the bus to Belize, then sell it there and be done with it.

When I crossed over into Mexico, there was some discussion about which form I should have. In the end, the officials prepared my papers and sent me on my way.

Then, at the first checkpoint, there was no problem. But at the second, they told me that I had the wrong papers.

An official proceeded to inspect the bus. I had two forty-five-gallon drums of gasoline on board. Since the fuel in Mexico was about a hundred fifty percent more expensive at that time, I had been trying to save some money.

The official asked me what I had in the drums. When I told him, he said sarcastically, "Don't you realize that they also sell gasoline here in Mexico?"

I smiled and said nothing.

Then a fully dressed officer entered the bus and asked, "What is going on here?"

The first man reiterated the issue with the papers and added, "But it seems that the people at the border wanted to do this person a favour."

With that, the second officer turned and left without saying another word. Instead of sending me back to the border, he seemed to be looking for some renumeration. He asked for a couple of bus seats and I agreed to let him have them.

It was clear sailing at last. I had a pretty good trip down. On the way, I happened to notice some migrating birds crossing over the road. They seemed to come in an everlasting trail. I couldn't help but wonder how long this seemingly continuous stretch of birds really was.

Then there was another surprise trail, but this time it was made up of yellow butterflies. They flew low at three to four feet above the ground, and I enjoyed watching them cross the road in front of me as I drove along.

Suddenly, I looked down at my dash and saw that the water temperature had risen up into the red line. I pulled over quickly and stopped.

When I came around to the front to open the engine hood, I noticed that the radiator was completely covered with yellow butterflies. I hadn't considered such a thing was possible! After I scraped off the blanket of butterflies and restarted the bus, the engine cooled down straightaway.

When I had about four hundred miles left to drive before reaching the border with Belize, I started to feel apprehensive about what difficulty I might encounter.

"Lord, open the door for me," I prayed as I drove down the highway.

After a bit, I felt a sense of confidence come over me that God had answered my prayer. I can't really describe it any better than that. I felt that if I truly believed that God had answered my prayer, I shouldn't let it continue to bother me. I struggled to push it out of my mind.

"Thank you, Lord," I said, dismissing my concern.

I arrived at the border and found a spot where I could park the bus. I casually put together my papers, trying desperately not to be nervous.

TWENTY-SIX: BACK FOR THE BUS

I stepped out of the bus and walked, like a stick man, to the immigration office. There was only one officer on duty and he was in discussion with another traveller. I politely stayed a distance away so as not to show any urgency on my part.

Eventually the officer reached out his hand in my direction, requesting my papers, while continuing his discussion with the other man. I handed him my papers and he drew an X on a line where he wanted me to sign. After signing and giving them back to him, he said, "Okay."

Surprised, I asked whether I was to go. "Is that all?"

"Yes, that is all," he said.

I tried to walk back out as casually as I had come in, but at the same time I wanted to hurry, in case somehow he changed his mind.

God had truly answered prayer. The door had indeed been opened wide for me to leave the country. I was soon cleared to enter Belize, and within a few more hours I was in Blue Creek.

However, the saga with the bus was not over. Four days after I arrived, I decided to take the bus to Orange Walk to see if I could find a buyer. But first it needed to be filled up with gas at the village store. To get there, I needed to drive up an escarpment that went from about fifty feet above sea level to about five hundred feet. The road was narrow with sharp curves and some places were only wide enough for one vehicle.

I got to the store and fuelled up. But while heading back down, the brake pedal went to the floor. I couldn't believe anything would have gone wrong with the brakes after serving me so well for some five thousand miles—and on two occasions they had saved me from certain collisions.

I was able to force the bus into gear, but not as low a gear as I would have liked. I put one hand on the horn while steering with the other, hoping that if someone was coming up and heard the horn he might pull over at a wide point in the road so I could pass. I felt that if I were to face a certain collision, I would have no choice but to steer the bus over the bank, where I could tumble for a hundred feet or more.

I made it down past the steepest and most treacherous part of the road and then remembered that if I turned off the key, the vehicle would slow down even more. I knew there was a ninety-degree turn at the bottom, which many a truck driver never made. Many with hot brakes would barrel through the barbed-wire fence and out onto the level pasture, but I now had control of the vehicle and made it to a stop on the side of the road without any mishap, praise the Lord.

My first thought was that God must have something more that he wanted me to do.

I examined the brake line and found that one clamp had broken off, allowing the line to vibrate against the side of the frame. Where it chafed, the line had worn paper thin. The line had rusted while the bus sat in high humidity for four days, making it easier for the brake line to split open. This bus didn't have a double brake system as all vehicles have today.

I repaired the line and parked the bus for a while. When I checked it again, a serious noise was coming from the engine. I pulled it apart only to discover that my make-do fix on the bearings had only lasted until I got to Belize. The rod bearing, which had scoring on the crank, now spun around. To sell the bus, I would have to grind the crank. Where could I get it ground? The nearest place was four hundred miles away at Villahermosa, Mexico.

A bit reluctantly, I put the crank in a feed bag and caught a ride to Chetumal. There I bought a ticket for Villahermosa, but the next three buses were all full. I had a four-hour wait.

As I walked around the bus station, I noticed an old colony Mennonite in his overalls waiting as well. When I got a chance, I spoke to him in Spanish. I asked where he was going, to which he answered, "Villahermosa." It turned out that we would be riding on the same bus.

I explained the reason for my trip and he pointed to another spot on the floor where there was another feed bag—and, guess what, a crank was inside. Not only were we going to the same place, on the same bus, but also for the same reason.

Eventually we caught our bus, but not before we discovered one more coincidence; our tickets seated us side by side. We talked throughout the journey.

TWENTY-SIX: BACK FOR THE BUS

When we arrived, we got rooms in a hotel to pass the night. Then, in the morning, we decided to go together to choose a machine shop to get our work done. We chose different shops, though, because his crank was from a diesel engine while mine was from a gasoline engine. We both bought oversized bearings to fit the cranks according to the new specs and went shopping to gather some other necessities.

We caught an early bus back to Chetumal the following day, and again we were seated side by side and had considerable time to talk.

I had a tremendous opportunity to share with this man. He had a strong religious background but didn't have a practical, everyday trust in the Lord.

A bus service would take us from Chetumal to the Belizean border, but from there on we had to try to catch a ride somehow. We sat for quite a long while waiting for just such an opportunity, and I prayed for God to provide for our immediate need.

While praying, a man came by in a pickup and offered us a ride to Orange Walk.

On the way I shared with this Mennonite man how God had answered prayer for us.

We still had quite a long way to travel, but before long we found another ride, this time as far as August Pine Ridge, on another truck.

Then we sat again for a long time. It would soon be dark. We met two other Mennonites there, waiting for a ride in their overalls.

Again I prayed for our trip home—and as I prayed, I heard a truck in a distance. The roads had so many potholes that the truck took quite a while to get to where we were.

I recognized the driver from Blue Creek, so I was quite sure he would give us a ride the rest of the way. However, my Mennonite friend made no move to get up.

The driver had stopped his truck and went straight into a nearby store for a refreshment. I thought that maybe my companion didn't think this driver would give us a ride.

I went inside the store and asked the driver if he would give us a ride to Blue Creek.

"Sure!" he said.

When I came back out to tell my friend the good news, he still made no move. I stared at him until finally it clicked: old colony Mennonites weren't allowed to have anything to do with excommunicated Mennonites. And even though it was getting late, there were two other Mennonites here who could pass on word to their church leaders that he had taken a ride.

"Well," I said, "I'm going to take this ride."

"Sure," he said. "You go right ahead."

I climbed on board, and a bit after dark I got home. I found out later that these Mennonites didn't get picked up until about 11:00 p.m. I felt sorry for them, but even more I wondered whether that man I had travelled with ever managed to differentiate between religion and a personal relationship with Jesus.

I could say in hindsight that I had a lot of difficulties with the school bus, but God was with me throughout all my trials. Someday maybe we will see fruit from this saga.

I reassembled the bus's motor and left the vehicle to sit in a field for some time, as I was occupied with other things.

Then I got a call one day from the owner of a busing company. He wanted to buy the bus. Of course, he wanted to beat me down, but my price wasn't high compared to all that I had done to it. I told him that if he didn't want it at my price, I would use it for a dwelling. After all, I didn't have a place of my own at the time. I would just build a roof over it to reduce the effect the intense heat of the sun.

Eventually, this man gave in to my price—perhaps because, as I heard later, several of his buses were broken down.

Twenty-Seven

WHAT DO I DO NOW LORD?

I had been in Belize now for several months, not knowing what God wanted me to do there. It seemed as though God had led me to Belize without giving me any direction. It was an anxious time for me and I took trips down to the southern tip of Belize, trying to assess the need and recognize God's voice.

Through it all, I kept reminding myself: *The Lord knows the way through the wilderness and all I have to do is follow.* I also meditated on the words of **Psalm 27:14:** *"Wait on the Lord: be of good courage, and He shall strengthen your heart: wait, I say, on the Lord!"* (NKJV)

I felt like a soldier marking time, raising my feet as though to march but returning them to the same position again. Soldiers wait for a command to move forward. They are at the ready, just like I was ready to respond to whatever God wanted me to do.

I was a bit surprised one day when Henry told me that the evangelical Mennonite church had a boat and an outboard motor they were willing to loan us so we could visit villages along the river if we wanted. The river was the boundary between Belize and Mexico, with the closest villages being on the Mexican side. I didn't hesitate to go along with the plan to share the gospel in this area.

We got the boat ready and headed downriver. After about three quarters of an hour, we came to a sizeable village called Botes. We made a number of attempts to share the gospel, but no one seemed very interested. One man told us that he didn't want to hear from the Bible because he figured the more he heard from the Bible, the greater he might be condemned later on when judgment came. He didn't realize that the wages of sin is death, and we are all condemned to die unless we receive the gift of God, which is eternal life through faith in the work of Christ on the cross of Calvary. There is no lesser condemnation.

We visited Botes a few times without any real opportunity to share the gospel. On our third trip, we realized that we had passed a much smaller village on the way, called Calderón. This village was on my mind when Henry suggested we stop there.

We tied the boat and made our way up the bank towards a level sports field close to the river's edge. The village could be seen in the distance. The roofs of the houses were all made from palm leaves and vertical posts lined the sides of the huts to keep out unwanted animals. All the houses had mud floors.

Before proceeding, we stopped to pray.

When we opened our eyes, we spotted a man walking into his house. We decided to visit this house first.

Upon arrival, we had to stoop down quite low to enter the doorway. The Mayan people are naturally very short-statured.

We introduced ourselves and stated that we had come to share the gospel of Jesus Christ. The man of the house certainly didn't want to appear interested in the gospel, so he said that he had an aunt who was interested in that sort of thing. He led us to her hut but then stayed to listen to what we had to say.

Many others soon gathered around until the hut was quite full. We sang a few choruses before Henry delivered a short message from the Bible.

After we prayed, we began to make our way to the door.

TWENTY-SEVEN: WHAT DO I DO NOW LORD?

"When are you coming back?" the aunt said loud enough for everyone to hear.

No sweeter words could have been spoken. They were like music to our ears. It was exactly what we wanted to hear and we quickly made a promise to return the following week.

The man of that house ended up being the first person in the village to accept Jesus as his Lord and Saviour. He was also one of the first to be baptized, and he later was the one to pastor the church in Calderón for years to come. Before we came to the village, he had been having bad experiences due to his drinking habits; he had already been thinking that perhaps he needed to seek God. At that point in his life, however, he hadn't known how to do it. I believe that the timing of our coming was critical for this man in particular. I have no doubt that God had led us there.

This man was one of the first to accept the Lord from his village and eventually became a pastor for the church in his village in Calderón, Mexico

Twenty-Eight

THE OLD COLONY MENNONITES OF BLUE CREEK

When I first came to live in Belize, I was given the use of an abandoned house to live in. Why was it abandoned? There were two reasons, and to explain it I will need to get into the Mennonite history of Blue Creek.

Old colony Mennonites have always sought to settle in places where they could live by themselves so they could practice a lifestyle that resembled what it might have been like a hundred years ago or so. They hold to a strict code of living and practice their religion in a way that keeps them uncontaminated by the rest of the world.

These Mennonites worked mostly from the land and sold the produce. Some dedicated themselves to a trade, like mechanics or carpentry, that was a benefit to the community. Most of the Mennonites from Blue Creek had moved from Chihuahua, Mexico. The colony in Chihuahua had gotten very large and some of them had been looking for a new place to start afresh.

A group of Mennonite leaders approached the Belizean government to request a large piece of unsettled jungle they could lease and eventually buy. Once they had established the lease, groups of families came and each was given a forty-acre lot. They had to quickly build a house to live in, then start clearing the jungle to be able to start planting and raising animals to make a living. The leaders were paid a yearly due which in turn went to the government to pay down the lease.

Life was difficult in these early years, but the land was quite productive and the Mennonites were hard-working.

Over time, tensions arose over certain issues. But as has been proven by history, a strict code of ethics doesn't change people's hearts towards God.

Evangelical Mennonite missionaries started visiting the colony teaching the gospel of Jesus Christ. The people began to see that religion couldn't save them, but having faith in the one who had died on the cross of Calvary could.

Many left the old colony church and started coming to the Evangelical Mennonite church. As soon as they did, they were excommunicated from the old colony church.

As time went on, so many Mennonites had left the old colony church that the remaining ones were advised by their leaders to sell and move away. By 1974, when I came to Belize, many old colony Mennonites were selling their properties and moving to other parts of Belize where new colonies had formed, or to other countries where a colony was established.

Some of these Mennonites who left the old colony had prospered quite well, so they would buy up the vacant properties to expand their farms. Since they already had houses and didn't have need for more, certain homes became abandoned.

That's how I came to acquire the house I lived in.

At that time, a few of the old colony people were working on their papers to move to another country, like Bolivia. They weren't allowed to own any vehicle other than a horse and cart, and their tractors couldn't have rubber tires.

TWENTY-EIGHT: THE OLD COLONY MENNONITES OF BLUE CREEK

Since there was no bus service back then and they weren't allowed to take rides from excommunicated Mennonites, they often asked if I would drive them to the city so they could work on their papers. Sometimes I drove as many as ten Mennonites to the city, and most of them sat on planks in the back of the pickup. This gave me the unique privilege of sharing the gospel with them.

Since our trips to the city could take five hours or more, we usually had to spend the night there, and I always stayed at the same place where most of the Mennonite went.

One night while staying overnight in the city, I got to sharing the gospel with three teenaged boys. They listened intently, as though they had never heard the gospel before.

One of the boys had only a limited knowledge of Spanish, less than the other two, so he often interrupted in Low German to ask, "What did he say?" I would then stop and wait for the other two to explain what I had just said.

I never expected that I would ever see any of these people again, especially since they were about to leave the country. In their case, they were headed to Bolivia.

Well, I went to an auction years later, and amongst the crowd stood a young man who was looking at me and smiling. I didn't know him, but he appeared to know me.

When we started talking, he spoke about an occasion in Belize City when I'd gotten into a discussion with him and two other teenagers. That's when I recognized him. I couldn't believe that he was one of those three boys! He hadn't done so well in Bolivia and had decided to come back to Belize.

Not only did that conversation leave an impact, but I believe that since that night he has trusted Christ as his personal Saviour.

Twenty-Nine

UNA COMPAÑERA
1975

As you might have guessed, I was still single at this time in my life. But the Teigrobs had told me about an English girl who had gone to Africa to help out the missionaries there to provide medical care. Henry and Anne knew about her from their letters with the Stanleys, a family they had been close friends with since they'd gone to missionary boot camp together. The Lord seemed to have led the two families in opposite directions, with the Teigrobs going to Central Americans and the Stanleys to West Africa.

This girl in West Africa didn't have a husband, according to Jim Stanley, and Henry had told him about me. Jim had been earnestly trying to get Henry to convince me to start writing letters to this girl. But what kind of guy would write to a girl he didn't know on the other side of the world? No one.

However, if you get a dig in the ribs enough times, you'll probably do something about it given enough time.

Finally, I agreed to write her, but I didn't want this girl to think I had an easy-going lifestyle. If I was going to begin a relationship with someone, she needed to be at home living in the jungle. I knew there were lots of missionaries who didn't live quite as crudely as I did, but I knew nothing about how she was living in Africa.

I must say, I wasn't just a bit surprised when she returned my letter. In it, she painted a picture that almost matched the one I had sent her.

After that, we began corresponding back and forth across the "pond."

I had also been writing another girl I knew from Costa Rica, but I didn't want to be writing to two girls at the same time unless they both knew about it. I wanted to communicate with them in all openness so there wouldn't be any surprises.

I sent off a pair of letters, in them explaining to each girl about the other person. I didn't know what the impact might be, but I trusted God for the outcome.

The girl in Costa Rica was very upset. After answering my letter, we didn't hear from each other again.

The girl in Africa didn't get the letter, so she didn't get upset. The letter strangely disappeared.

Again, as the saying goes, *The Lord knows the way through the wilderness and all I have to do is follow.* God works out the details for us!

Grace and I continued to write to each other and eventually came to believe that God had independently answered our prayers. We both became convinced that God was directing us to come together in marriage and work together for God's kingdom.

Now what plans should we make? I felt it would only be right for Grace's family to have the privilege of being part of our marriage ceremony, since she would soon be living away from her homeland. So we decided that she would return to her home in England to arrange for the wedding. I planned to meet her there, and after we married we would briefly stop by to visit my folks in Canada before continuing to Belize.

You must realize that communication back then was nothing like what it is today. Snail mail, or letter-writing, was the only option. It took close to two weeks for a letter to travel from Belize to Senegal. Then

TWENTY-NINE: UNA COMPAÑERA

that letter had to take a long journey to Tambacounda, where it sat until someone made a special trip from Kedougou, where she was staying, to pick it up.

Her reply, of course, would take an equally long time to return.

We trusted God for a lot of the type of issues that are normally sorted out in courtship, believing that he would work out those details. For instance, how old was the other person? Were they good-looking? I did have an edge on her because she had sent me a picture in the mail. By the time I had one to send to her, it was close to the time when she would be departing for England and it might not have gotten to her place in the jungle in time.

Therefore, I sent my picture to England so at least she might recognize me when she had to pick me up at the airport.

We came up with a wedding date of September 6, so I would try to get to England by then.

Grace knew I had limited funds and wanted to send money so I wouldn't have any difficulty with the expenses. I refused, since I was trusting God; if he was really leading us together, he would supply me with enough money to get to England.

I had another issue at stake. It had been two years since I had left Costa Rica, and the people there had expected me to come back.

While living in Costa Rica, I had noticed a problem wherein some of the Maleku farmers had trouble trying to get started in raising cattle. They first had to clear jungle and plant grass for the pasture. Then they had to gather money to buy heifers. Before the heifers reached an age where they could have calves, sickness or other mishaps often struck the farmers or their families, forcing them to sell the heifers. Sometimes they would end up right back where they had started.

I had thought of a plan to help one particular man. I would buy the heifer for what it was worth at the time and he could continue raising it, with me taking a partial share. He liked the idea and he was able to start increasing the number of his animals.

Another person was desperate for money and offered to sell me a plot of land so he could get out of a financial dilemma. I didn't know what I would use the lot for, but I had thought I could sell one day later on.

There was yet another woman who had wanted to buy a piglet, so she could raise it to sell when it had grown up—but she didn't have any money. She pleaded with me to buy the piglet for her and we would, again, share ownership. I wasn't in it for the money. I just bought it to help her out.

This is why I needed to return for at least a short visit and to share how God had led me to a ministry in Belize. I was getting letters about the land and the animals I partially owned.

I wasn't concerned about these investments, since I had been pleased to help these people, hoping above all else that they would accept and follow the Lord, who is our provider. But they were quite a bit more concerned about returning to me what they believed I was owed.

I looked into the cost of tickets and found that the price of flights lowered considerably at the beginning of September. Therefore I decided to travel from Belize to Costa Rica in the latter part of August, planning to fly to England in early September.

When I got to Costa Rica, I concentrated first and foremost on the ministry of the gospel. I spent the first few days visiting villages and holding services in the evenings.

After making the rounds, so to speak, I paid attention to the concerns of these people who wished to settle their accounts.

The piglet had grown up and had a litter. The original piglet had been butchered, and now the litter, too, had grown and were all sold—except for two animals, and one of them had a broken leg. They found a buyer for the remaining pig in good health and gave me the proceeds of the sales. I really hadn't expected anything in return, but for the sake of their consciences, I accepted what they gave me. I knew God would bless them for their honesty and integrity.

The man who had sold me the plot of land now had the money to buy it back, which took care of that issue.

As for the man whom I'd helped get started in cattle-raising, he was desperately looking for a buyer for one of his heifers. He had found a prospective buyer, but this man wouldn't be able to come until Friday, the day I expected to leave. If I waited one more day in the expectation that the heifer would sell, I would have a very tight schedule to get back to San José.

For Leonel's benefit, I chose to wait and leave the following day.

The money, I felt, was no issue. But before God, this brother wanted to settle his accounts.

There was one more detail—small in the grand scheme of things, yet big for me—that never left my mind. I knew a man, named Luis, who was pleased to hear that I was going to England to get married. He reached into his pocket and pulled out fifty colonies—approximately four dollars—to give me for my upcoming trip. That wasn't much money to me, but it was a lot for a Costa Rican, and even more for the Maleku, considering their poverty.

Thirty

IS THAT MAN GOING TO SHOW UP OR NOT?

Once I had everything taken care of in the palenques, I left early, on Saturday morning, to get to the airstrip in Guatuso. I wanted to get on the list for the first plane out. Three planes were scheduled to depart for Ciudad Quesada that day, and I managed to get booked on the first plane.

For some reason, though, a smaller plane arrived on the grass landing strip than expected and it could only take three passengers instead of four. Guess who got bumped? Me, of course.

You would think I would be the first on the list for the next flight, but no, the "gringo" would have to wait until the last flight of the day.

The Lord knows the way through the wilderness and all I have to do is follow.

I just needed to wait on the Lord.

As soon as I landed, I took a taxi to the bus station in order to catch a bus for San José.

It was past noon before I got to the capital. Now, when I got close to my travel agent's office, I noticed that all the offices were closed. I made a real effort to contact the travel agent at his home, with the hope that maybe he could do something special for me, but I couldn't reach him.

Finally, I relaxed and decided to leave it in God's hands. Instead I went out to visit my friend Francisco from Tonjibe, who was attending Bible school in Liberia, a three-hour bus ride from San José. I had been unable to see him while I was in the palenques because he was in the city preparing for the ministry.

I got back to San José on Sunday evening and again tried to call the travel agent at his home. I was pleased to hear his voice when he answered. He had waited at his office the previous day until 1:00 p.m., expecting me to show up. When I hadn't come, he had left for the weekend.

We must have just missed each other.

"It's not a problem, though," he told me. "There is an afternoon flight to Miami. It will arrive in time for you to still catch your flight to London."

That was a relief! He told me to come into his office at 8:00 a.m.

When I entered his office the next morning, he was in a terrible dither.

"Don, I just realized that there is no afternoon flight to Miami on Mondays," he said first thing. "What are you going to do?"

"Well, put me on the flight for tomorrow," I replied calmly.

He grabbed the phone and started making the arrangements. When he got off the phone, he asked me to come back in the afternoon.

But I now had a different concern that was giving me butterflies. I didn't know for sure if I had enough money to pay for the flight. I asked the agent to give me a total of how much it was all going to cost.

Back at the hotel, I counted all the money I had—wondering, of course, if I shouldn't have taken up Grace's offer to help—and praise the Lord, I had just enough for the travel agent, the hotel, the bus fare to the airport, and still enough to send a night letter to England so Grace wouldn't be expecting me until September 3, instead of September 2 as we had planned.

I felt quite relieved.

The next morning, I got on the bus for the airport at 4:00 a.m. and was surprised to find the terminal crowded with far more people than one would expect at such an early hour. I noticed a sign up on the wall stating in large print that everyone would have to pay an airport terminal tax.

Seeing the amount, I realized that I no longer had enough money left over to cover this unexpected expense. What an embarrassment! Here I was supposed to fly to England and I wasn't able to pay the airport terminal tax! What was I going to do?

I walked up and down the corridors of the terminal, dodging my way through the crowd.

"Lord, you brought me this far," I prayed. "I know you won't let me down at this stage. I am your royal subject, and it would not be the royal way to ask someone to give me money for this tax…"

Suddenly, God jogged my memory.

Two years earlier, when I had been back in Nova Scotia preparing to go south with the bus, the Wittenburg Baptist Church had given me a going away card. When I had opened the card, I had found $31 inside. Since it was a small amount, I had closed up the card and put it in a safe place in my luggage. I had completely forgotten about that money until I had been sifting through my belongings in Belize, trying to sort out what I should take with me to Costa Rica and later to England.

When I came across this card, I put the money aside for a rainy day, and now it was pouring buckets.

"Thank you, Lord!" I said.

I still had one small problem. The money was in Canadian dollars, and the banks weren't yet open for me to make the exchange. Besides, Canadian dollars weren't readily exchangeable.

Finally, I decided to ask a teller at a small trinket shop. Did she know where I could possibly exchange $31 Canadian?

"I don't know what the exchange rate is," she said.

I told her what the exchange rate had been the last time I had need to exchange Canadian dollars into colonies. Without any farther hesitation, she agreed to this rate and dished out the equivalent amount in colonies.

Again, praise the Lord! The door was now fully open for me to fly to England.

You might be thinking I was completely broke by now, but that wasn't entirely true. I managed to find seventy American cents in the bottom of my satchel. And I needed every penny of it, since I had a ten-hour layover in Miami. Fortunately, back then they still served meals on the planes at no extra cost.

Still, I needed to plan wisely while in Miami. I sat calmly for the first five hours, then thought about how I might spend those seventy cents on something that would get me through the next five. I was too embarrassed to ask for the price of anything due to my situation, so I only stopped at places that had prices listed on the wall.

I finally found a place that sold a hot chocolate and a doughnut for seventy cents. Nowadays five dollars wouldn't buy that much at an airport terminal.

There were more holdups. After we boarded the plane, the captain's voice was heard over the loudspeakers announcing a delay. One of the starter motors of one of the engines was faulty and would have to be replaced. We remained seated in our places for the next hour. Then the captain spoke again, praising the mechanics for how fast they had been able to make the repair.

Not long after that, we were up in the air and on our way to England.

It seemed like a rather short night. Because we were flying east, the time zone change brought us four hours ahead.

As we approached London, we heard the captain's voice yet again, this time to inform us that because we had been late leaving Miami, we were no longer in sequence for the landing pattern. London Heathrow airport was so busy that we had to circle over the city at three or four thousand feet. We circled three times before the plane finally was given permission to enter the circuit pattern and come in for a landing.

On the ground, there was another problem: there was no ramp available to us. So we had to stop out on tarmac and wait for busses to transport us to the terminal. Our 747 was full and only two buses were dispatched. After the busses were full, they drove back to unload the passengers at the terminal only to return to reload. Since I was at the back of the plane, I was among the last to leave the plane. It took over an hour to unload the plane.

When I got to the terminal, it was packed with passengers from all sorts of different places. I followed the zigzag to get into the immigration line, feeling a bit weary and apprehensive about what questions the immigration official would ask me. I wondered if he might ask how much money I had on me to spend during my stay in England.

I needn't have worried about that. The immigration officer asked only one question: "What is your purpose for coming to England?"

"To get married."

Bang! He stamped my passport and handed it back. "That sounds like a good reason to me."

Now my concern was focused on Grace. I expected she would know that the plane had arrived late, but would she still be waiting two hours after the plane had landed for me to come through the doors?

Little did I know what hoops she had already gone through since I had sent that night letter from Costa Rica. A night letter, so I had been told, was a telegram that was supposed to be delivered immediately. However, it hadn't arrived at her family's home until ten o'clock the next morning.

Not only had Grace been at the airport, but she had been waiting at the arrival doors for quite a long time.

As she'd waited, at last she had heard her named called over the loudspeakers: "Grace Edwards, can you please come to the information desk?"

Thinking that somehow she must have missed me coming through the doors, she hurried as quickly as she could to the information desk. The woman there asked if she was waiting for her fiancé.

"Yes," she answered.

"Well, he's not coming. Your mother has a message for you: he has been delayed for another day."

Poor Grace! What was she to do? Go back to Southampton and come back in the morning? That would require four hours of travel.

She had a friend living in London who was happy to put her up for the night and save her the trip back to her parents' place. However, she hadn't known that the next day's flight from Miami had been delayed until she got to the airport, and that it would be at least three more hours before I got off the plane was processed through customs.

Finally, though, the wait was over and we saw each other for the first time. How do two strangers say hello?

Well, there wasn't much time for that business.

"We have to go quickly to Southampton to the registrar," Grace told me.

I didn't understand it, but I jumped into action. I followed her to the parking lot where she led me to a little black car that I thought looked like an antique.

"What, you drive this?" I said.

She didn't know what to make of my exclamation. She was as surprised at me as I was surprised at her car.

Actually, it wasn't as old as it first appeared to be. Cars in England were noticeably smaller than the average in North America, partly because the price of fuel was considerably higher in England. The car was also in immaculate condition.

Grace was soon whizzing down the highway on the wrong side of the road. Good thing I wasn't driving, because all the other cars were on the wrong side of the road as well. Every time I opened my eyes and saw a car coming my heart skipped a beat. I wanted to see all the new and different scenery, but the traffic scared me.

Nevertheless, we had to hurry to the registrar's office. Why? Grace explained that we had to sign the marriage declaration seventy-two hours before the wedding could take place. We had no time to spare.

We arrived at the registrar's office at 4:30 p.m., just in time.

The registrar would have to be present to hear the vows, so he offered some times for when the wedding could take place. He had only two times available on September 6, though: 9:00 a.m. or 5:00 p.m. Grace chose 5:00 p.m.

God's hand again was evident, because we had arrived at the registrar's office precisely thirty minutes before the seventy-two-hour deadline started.

Now we could relax a bit as we headed to the Edwards homestead.

That afternoon, Grace's mom had gone out to close the gate at the end of their lane.

"Don't close the gate," her father had said. "I have faith that Grace's man is still going to come."

And he finally did.

When we arrived at 8 Pound Road, I had a bunch of new faces to get to know. So many things were different. Even the language was hard to understand. Yes, they spoke English… but when they talked among themselves, I often couldn't catch what they were saying.

But one thing was for sure: I was warmly welcomed by all of Grace's family and friends, and that is still true today.

However, I wasn't allowed to stay at the homestead for night. I wouldn't stay there until after the wedding. Grace's dear Aunt Dorthey put me up for the next three days.

Our wedding was special. Many believing friends offered to help with different aspects of the wedding. Someone also offered to take care of all the photography. Plus, Middle Road Baptist Church kindly offered their church for the wedding. The pastor, Mr. Tony Knight, who had overseen the gifts given to Grace while on the mission field, officiated our wedding and continued to serve in that capacity for our mission work Central America.

Another church offered their hall for our reception. More than two hundred people came to the wedding and the reception afterwards. Some had come to see Grace getting married while others wanted to see this man who she was hitching up with, a man she had courted only by mail and whom she hadn't seen until three days before the wedding.

There was no debt involved with this wedding. Someone offered us a place to stay on the Isle of White at a Christian guest home for our honeymoon. We needed this time to get to know one another.

After the wedding was over, we felt overwhelmed by all the blessings that had been piled upon us. We finally got into the car and drove to the docks to catch the ferry. Many followed to see us off.

Grace wanted me to drive, even though I hadn't driven on the wrong side of the road before. I don't know who was more afraid, me or her.

When we got there, it seemed that the ferry had been waiting for us because it left as soon as we got on board.

The Isle of White didn't have much traffic, which was a good thing. There were many road changes and every time I made a turn I naturally moved to the right side of the road only to be told that this was the wrong side.

We spent several days at the guest home and seeing the many sights on the island. The owners offered to let us stay the entire week at no cost, but we needed to go. We were planning to spend some time in Canada next to visit my folks before driving back to Belize.

Grace and I

THIRTY: IS THAT MAN GOING TO SHOW UP OR NOT?

Just after we were married

Grace and her parents by her little car

CONCLUSION

To summarize, I would say first that there are many more stories I could have shared about the ministry Grace and I shared in Belize and Mexico. However, this book was focused more on my time in Costa Rica.

Grace later joined me on trips to Costa Rica to see firsthand how the believers there were maturing in their faith.

The stories in this book testify to how God was a help in real life situations. I lacked a lot of faith, but in obeying God according to his word and promptings he met me where the rubber grips the road.

In the Bible, there's a story in which one of Abraham's servants, believing God would guide him, obeyed and went off to find a wife for Isaac. After praying for guidance in who to choose, God answered.

The servant said, *"I being in the way, the Lord led me to the house of my master's brethren"* (Genesis 24:27).

God offers the same guidance for us. As it says in Hebrews 13:8, *"Jesus Christ is the same yesterday, today, and forever"* (NKJV).

I trust that these real life stories of God's hand in the work of building His church in Costa Rica among the Maleku will be an encouragement to others. It has not been an easy road and tears have been shed along the way, but despite all the discouragements and difficulties, it was a privilege to be a part of what took place in that little area of the world.

Today well over half of the Maleku confess Jesus Christ as their Lord and Saviour, glory to God.

The Teigrobs and myself may have played a part in the start-up of the church of Jesus Christ, but others watered the work that we began. The people themselves did a lot of planting and watering even well beyond their communities.

Although I only lived there for a few years between 1968 and 1973, I visited from time to time afterward. I no longer shed so many tears of sorrow, but rather I have shed tears of joy in amazement for what God continues to do there.

My experience of God's work in Costa Rica has been my greatest encouragement during my time ministering in Belize and Mexico, and also during the years I spent back in Canada. I am so glad that I went. I think of how different life for me would have been if I had not taken God seriously. I wish God's richest blessings on all those who appreciate this testimony.

ABOUT THE AUTHOR

After finishing high school, Don Dodsworth trained as an electronic technician at HMS Dockyard in Halifax between 1964 and 1968. After deciding to go to Costa Rica, he picked up a working knowledge of mechanics, largely influenced by Henry Teigrob, the missionary he worked with. Having grown up on a farm, and later working with his father in carpentry work, Don gained a practical knowledge in many areas of expertise.

Even though he didn't have any formal Bible training, he learned to trust in God and the Bible in a very literal sense through Henry's example. And while struggling to learn Spanish, he spent many hours in Bible reading and study.

On Don's first trip home in the spring of 1970, he acquired an electrical qualification and got a job as an electrician. At the same time, he trained to earn a private pilot's license.

In 1975, he married a missionary from England, Grace, who was a nurse and midwife working in Senegal. Grace soon came to operate a medical clinic in Blue Creek, Belize. Together, Grace and Don worked as a team, often flying people into the city who had medical emergencies too serious to be cared for at the clinic.

Their main ministry involved church-planting in the Spanish communities in both Belize and Mexico.

As their three children grew older into their high school years, Grace and Don decided to move back to Canada in the fall of 1988 for their children's higher education.

Don's work varied greatly from that point on, although he continued to visit the believers in Belize and Mexico on an almost annual basis—and more sporadically in Costa Rica. He worked as an industrial electrician and later worked in computer assembly and repair. He eventually made a big change and went into long-haul trucking for fifteen years.

Throughout these careers, God has given him many opportunities to share the gospel. Sadly, Grace fell ill with cancer and has gone home to be with the Lord.

In later life, Don taught himself programming and programmed LED signs for a Bible camp and a church in Mexico. The main objective has been to put Scripture on display. He recently upgraded that program and has created a new font that is bolder yet not too large to display a number of words per line.

Don continues to look for ways to serve and share his testimony. He claims that he is still learning how to follow the Lord through the wilderness.

Milton Keynes UK
Ingram Content Group UK Ltd.
UKHW02081817I123
432750UK00018B/924